C000141510

AS SAFE AS HOUSES

Cracking the Code to Profitable Property Investment

SILAS J. LEES

As Safe As Houses

First published in 2015 by

Panoma Press Ltd.
St Vincent Drive, St Albans, Herts, AL1 5SJ, UK
info@panomapress.com
www.panomapress.com

Book design and layout by Neil Coe.

Printed on acid-free paper from managed forests.

ISBN 978-1-784520-74-8

The right of Silas J. Lees to be identified as the author of this work has been asserted in accordance with sections 77 and 78 of the Copyright Designs and Patents Act 1988.

A CIP catalogue record for this book is available from the British Library.

This book is available online and in bookstores.

Dedication

I dedicate this book to all those people who are determined enough to make their dreams come true. Those of you who continually face uphill struggles, setbacks and disappointments in life, yet keep on going no matter what. The road to personal success is long and winding, full of learning opportunities, which bring certain challenges and frustrations. However, those determined souls who keep digging deep and keep trying 'just one more time' know that one day soon, it will all be worthwhile. You are the true heroes in life, and my inspiration.

Thank you for being all that you are. x

Testimonials

"No nonsense, how-to guide for serious property investors only. No fluff here!"

Adrian Pickersgill

"What the book 'Rich Dad Poor Dad' doesn't teach you about property investing and passive income is all revealed here!"

Tommy Franzén

"This book gave me the real deal by cutting through the smoke and mirrors surrounding the world of property investing."

Suzanne El-Shazly

"It's not a book... it's an instruction manual for property investment!"

Greg Ellis

Acknowledgments

There have been many people who have touched and shaped my life in some way, especially those people I have worked closely with throughout my journey in property investment as a trainer and personal property mentor. Your personal stories, backgrounds and 'reasons why' inspire me every single day to be the best that I can be to serve you better in what I do. Thank you. x

I could not write this book and be the person that I am today without acknowledging my two entrepreneur heroes: Donald Trump and Richard Branson. Through your books and actions, you have both inspired me greatly to follow in your footsteps to be the best that I can be. Thank you. x

There have been a number of organisations as well as coaches and mentors who have helped me significantly overcome my own internal barriers and conflicts, and for this I am very grateful. I certainly haven't got life all figured out, however, the following people and organisations have definitely helped me to gain a greater insight and understanding into who I am, and achieve success in life. I would like to extend significant thanks to Landmark Worldwide for creating The Landmark Forum and for helping me overcome obstacles that held me back for 25 years, and rebuild my family and personal life; the late Jim Rohn for your powerful teachings and strategies for helping me live a good life; David Foster, E-Myth Coach and the most powerful personal mentor I have ever experienced in my life – thank you for your support and guidance in this journey; Robert Kiyosaki and the Tigrent/Rich Dad Organisation who have helped me learn many powerful investment strategies and mould me into the successful investor, mentor and speaker I am today; and finally Mindy Gibbins-Klein who has guided me through this project to ensure I got this book written and published to launch a new career as an author! Thank you. x

There are also those people who have touched my life very deeply and personally helped to shape and mould me into the person that I am today. I would specifically like to acknowledge Randall and Alana Wright, Carl and Miki Wetherill, as well as Adrian and Clare Pickersgill for being very close friends and inspiring me more than you will ever know; Greg Ellis for your close companionship and friendship over the last seven years and guiding me through the darkest times in my life, as well as being a role model for leading a successful life; Suzy El-Shazly for your love, support, friendship and huge sense of fun, which have brought great joy and much happiness to my life – thank you for being all that you are. x

Finally, I most definitely wouldn't be where I am today without the nourishment I get from my family, and I would like to acknowledge them for their continuing love and support through my ups and downs in life, and for loving me when I was most un-loveable! Special thanks go to my two brothers, Gareth and Johnathan, who I will always love no matter what and whether I tell you often enough! And my dear parents who have been my role models and inspirations through life and taught me so many valuable life lessons and skills which have carried me far. I want you to know that you did an excellent job as parents and I love you with all my heart! Thank you, thank you, thank you. x

Contents

Disclaimer

This book is for information and an overview of the current property market only. My views, opinions and suggested strategies do not constitute financial advice in any way. You should always seek independent professional advice before making any investment. Like all investments, investing in property can be a risky business: recent growth in property prices and the rental market does not necessarily mean that prices will always increase in the future. Your property may be repossessed if you do not keep up payment on your mortgage.

CHAPTER ONE

Introduction - Why do you want to invest in property?

This is a serious question – why on earth would you want to buy property in the UK and rent it out? Or do it up and sell it on for a profit? What is it about buying property that we Brits idolise so much?

As a professional property investor myself, and someone who has spent the last seven years of my life helping educate other people to do the same in a safe and secure manner, I am always fascinated why people want to start the journey into buying property and renting it out. After all, there are plenty of other things that you could be doing with your time which are less stressful, more fun and less risky, so why would you want to go after buying property?

This is something that we are going to explore throughout this book, and, whilst it's something that you don't have to know or understand, if you *really* want to be successful at investing in property I would encourage you to look deeply at the reasons why you are doing so.

Over the years, I have met many people who dismiss the reason why they are choosing to invest in property as some 'Namby-Pamby American Psycho-Babble', citing that it does nothing to add value to their journey, as they just want to make more money. Whilst on the surface this might seem to be a good enough justification, pursuing something just for money's sake is ultimately deeply unfulfilling.

Unfortunately, it's the one thing that most people want more of. However, in my experience, just doing things for money alone will leave you empty and unfulfilled. I feel qualified to comment on this as money was my primary motivator for around 17 years – it left me feeling like there was never enough money for the things I wanted to do and ultimately I would not do *anything* unless there was a financial reward behind it. You can imagine how empty life was without the pursuit of hobbies and things of interest outside of work!

So, whilst money can be one motivator for some people, I ultimately believe there are many deeper and more fulfilling reasons why you are choosing to consider getting into property. Those people who dismiss this exercise (and I have met many of them) will usually be the ones who I meet a year or two later and are still 'thinking about doing something with property but are just "too busy" right now'. Right, you're too busy earning a living to think about making any real money?!

What is *your* reason for wanting to buy property? Are you tired of the lack of financial and/or job security? We are all aware of the impact the global recession which began in 2008 has had on the lives of those people around us, with some people losing their income overnight with the knock-on effects of their homes and livelihoods being in jeopardy.

Perhaps you are looking towards the future and retirement plans and you are concerned about the performance of your pension, or you don't have a pension at all. This can be a scary prospect for many people and it is interesting to note that most investors in property are men in their 40s and 50s. It would be logical to assume that these people are thinking about the future and realising that their pension left in the hands of others isn't performing anywhere as well as they had hoped (or had been suggested at the time when they took out the plan!). They may also be thinking about the 'final curtain', and wondering what is going to be left as a representation of their time on this earth. The desire to look after their children and provide for them is certainly strong, and the provision of a legacy in the form of income-producing assets for their children is certainly a big driver for some people.

A lasting income that produces a legacy is in stark contrast to where people's daily efforts in a job are rewarded in the form of a pay cheque at the end of the month, but in order to get the same reward, they must continue to invest the same 40-60-100 hours a week in their job looking after someone else's dreams! This reminds me of the time when I was working full-time in a job and my boss pulled up at work one morning in a brand new Range Rover. Now, being a bit of a fan of Range Rovers I couldn't help but stop and stare and tell my boss what a 'sweet ride' it was. My boss, being the kind guy that he was, said this to me: *"Thank you Silas. I'll tell you what; if you work really hard and put in all the extra hours, do lots of overtime and produce some great results, next year, **I'll** have an even better one..."* It was then that I realised the importance of looking after myself and my own dreams.

On that note, I am amazed at how many of us who had childhood dreams of what we wanted to do when we grew up; however, between childhood and early adulthood, it appears those dreams get sidelined or forgotten about, and most people condemn themselves to a lifetime of drudgery and routine in order to keep food on the table. I have my own theories on this; it's almost as if the education system kicks people's dreams out of them so that they will make faithful and regular employees, although I am sure this is not the case in reality...!

This is interesting to me as I meet many people in their 40s, 50s and 60s who say they wish they had had the courage to live out their dreams rather than working so hard in their jobs. In fact, there was a study carried out in 2013 by a nurse who cared for elderly people in their final months of life, and she compiled a list of the top five regrets of the dying (see: http://www.karenstan.net/2013/11/11/ nurse-reveals-top-5-regrets-people-make-deathbed   for more information). They were as follows (taken directly from the nurse's findings):

1. I wish I'd had the courage to live a life true to myself, not the life others expected of me.

This was the most common regret of all. When people realize that their life is almost over and look back clearly on it, it is easy to see how many dreams have gone unfulfilled. Most people had not honoured even half of their dreams and had to die knowing that it was due to choices they had made, or not made.

It is very important to try to honour at least some of your dreams along the way. From the moment that you lose your health, it is too late. Health brings a freedom very few realise, until they no longer have it.

2. I wish I didn't work so hard.

This came from every male patient that I nursed. They missed their children's youth and their partner's companionship. Women also spoke of this regret. But as most were from an older generation, many of the female patients had not been breadwinners. All of the men nursed deeply regretted spending so much of their lives on the treadmill of a work existence.

3. I wish I'd had the courage to express my feelings.

Many people suppressed their feelings in order to keep peace with others. As a result, they settled for a mediocre existence and never became who they were truly capable of becoming. Many developed illnesses relating to the bitterness and resentment they carried as a result.

4.   I wish I had stayed in touch with my friends.

Often they would not truly realise the full benefits of old friends until their dying weeks and it was not always possible to track them down. Many had become so caught up in their own lives that they had let golden friendships slip by over the years. There were many deep regrets about not giving friendships the time and effort that they deserved. Everyone misses their friends when they are dying.

5.   I wish that I had let myself be happier.

This is a surprisingly common one. Many did not realise until the end that happiness is a choice. They had stayed stuck in old patterns and habits. The so-called 'comfort' of familiarity overflowed into their emotions, as well as their physical lives. Fear of change had them pretending to others, and to their selves, that they were content. When deep within, they longed to laugh properly and have silliness in their life again. When you are on your deathbed, what others think of you is a long way from your mind. How wonderful to be able to let go and smile again, long before you are dying.

No matter what stage you are at in your life, the above makes stark reading for us all. I am so grateful that I made some serious changes in my life to allow me to pursue a life outside of the 9-5 daily grind. If you would like some extra motivation on finding your why, let me give you the following simple exercise:

1. Write down your monthly take-home pay.

2. Write down the number of hours you work every week. To my mind, the time you spend at work is calculated from the moment you wake up in the morning (as you are thinking about going to work and getting ready for the day), right through to the second you walk in through the front door in the evening (if you are someone who takes work home with you to do in the evening or you find yourself thinking/talking about work when you get home, count these hours too).

3. Multiply the hours in (2) above by 4.33 to give you a total monthly amount and write this down.

4. Divide the number you wrote down in (1) above by the number you worked out in (3) above. Write this figure down.

When you get to the end of (4) above, this is your hourly pay rate. So, for example, if you are earning the national average salary of around £26,500 and you are working 40 hours a week, wake up at 7am and get home at 7pm, then I would calculate this as follows:

1) £26,500 divided by 12 = £2,208.33 per month salary

2) 12 hours a day x 5 = 60 hours per week

3) 60 x 4.33 = 259.8 hours per month

4) £2,208.33 divided by 259.8 = £8.50 per hour.

The majority of people who do this exercise are staggered at how little they are earning. It also tends to be those people who are earning a seemingly decent salary in a profession who get the biggest shock, as higher earnings also usually carry an expectation that they work lots of long hours and do plenty of overtime. Of course, this is also without taking into account the slice of the pie that the tax authorities get their hands on before we receive our pay!

So, just how do we turn this situation around and increase our return on time invested? Well, from my point of view, there are many reasons why you want to consider investing in property:

- **Buy the right property and it will pay you for the rest of your life** – This is probably the single biggest reason why you should be investing in property and is one of the big reasons why I love property so much. Throughout this book, you will learn how to do this.

- **Create a retirement income… and enjoy it now** – The right property produces an investment income which you can live off now, rather than having to wait many years to take it in retirement.

- **Create a legacy for your family… or a charity** – The income produced from a property can be enjoyed for as long as you or your family own the property… *and* manage it correctly. This can be passed on to others once the final curtain falls.

- **Enjoy your income without having to go to work every day to create it** – The investment income nature of property allows you to be paid every month, as long as it is managed correctly. I like to think of it as 'Do the work once and get paid every single month… for the rest of your life!' Contrast this to the monthly effort required in a job and the longevity of the same income.

- **Time freedom** – When you are no longer having to trade your time for money, what is possible for you to achieve in your life? Perhaps you could do some 'far-out' things such as watch your kids grow up and spend time with the people you love, building quality relationships that really grow and nourish you, rather than chasing after those pieces of paper with the Queen's Head on them. Interestingly, I saw a picture of a bank note one day with a caption that said: *"I am a piece of paper and I control your whole life"*. That's something to think about!

- **Write your own income and become your own boss** – wouldn't it be liberating to give up your day job and say goodbye to your boss and all the frustrations that go with your day-to-day work life? Wouldn't it be fun to remove the glass ceiling on income and find a better view than looking up at someone else's bottom on the corporate ladder?

- **Help others more** – Most people I speak to would love to help other people more. My view is that charity begins at home and once you have taken care of yourself, your income and your future, you can help others in a very authentic manner.

- **Pursue your dreams** – Sounds idealistic doesn't it? Here's my question to you: *"If money was no obstacle to you, what would you do?"* Time to stop and think for a while – what would *you* do?

The last point is very much worthy of consideration. Most of us work in order to keep a roof over our heads and food on the table. If all that were taken care of for us each month, how would we spend our time?

Here's my final take on this – if you want it badly enough, you will find a way to make it happen. If you don't, you'll find an excuse. We all have reasons why we can't do something, from being too busy and not having enough time, to our everyday circumstances that prevent us from being able to go after what we want in life. If we choose to be limited by our present circumstances in life and the rulebook that we ourselves have created, then we are small people.

However, my belief is that every single one of us is a gifted person who is here on this earth to share their gift in some way and play as a 'big person' in the game of life. Some of us feel that because we can't excel at the world of sport or acting or singing and become famous worldwide, we should dismiss ourselves from being important and go on to lead a life that is less than fulfilling. As the saying goes: "Everyone has a gift, but some people choose not to open the package". We subconsciously beat ourselves up and play small at the game of life in all areas, thinking others are destined for greatness whilst we lead lives of quiet desperation.

Let me ask you this: *Would you be willing to invest the next few years of your life working on yourself and creating a property portfolio that will pay you for the rest of your life so that you can lead the life of your dreams?* If you choose not to, then there is no judgment here. Anyone can lead the life they want to; if you imagine lying on your deathbed looking back on your life, would you be happy with the results you created and the life you led, or would you regret not accomplishing more? Would you have some (or all) of the regrets listed earlier? If you feel you would, reflect on what the older version of you would say to yourself today about whether or not you are going to do this – there will be some pertinent advice and guidance there for you to reflect on and listen to. We just need to underpin a strong reason 'why' that will keep us going to the eventual end goal, so that we don't take ourselves out of the game and quit when the going gets tough.

To highlight this point, I'd like to introduce you to Mike. Mike had all the reasons in the world not to start a journey in property. He is the chief breadwinner in his household and he also has a terminally ill daughter and disabled wife for whom he is the chief carer. With all that going on in his life, it would have been very easy for Mike to make this his reason for not putting the time and effort into learning about property investment and building a property portfolio. Instead, he chose to live life as a 'big person' and made his family circumstances his 'why', so that he could create a portfolio providing investment income and not have to spend 40+ hours a week in an unfulfilling job when he could be with his family.

I'd also like to reference Fred and Wendy, whom I met a few years ago. They are a retired couple who had a burning desire to go and help women in Africa overcome serious and aggressive sexual assault. When I met them, they were in the process of selling their home in order to bank the money and then use this stockpile of cash to live off whilst they did their charity work. As much as I admired them for this, I suggested that they might want to invest the money they had into property, which would provide a lifetime income to support their charity work, otherwise they would have to come back to the UK once their money ran out. Not only did they take this advice on board and take action, they also went on to get help and assistance from a well-known member of Dragon's Den at a charity function we attended together. It's amazing what can happen when your desire is strong enough!

Both of these examples truly humble me and inspire me to play the game of life at a much bigger level. I hope they motivate and inspire you to take action towards your goals and dreams in life as – let's be realistic about it – the only person really stopping you getting what you want in life is the person looking at you in the mirror every morning! On that note, I would encourage you to write out your 'why' and put this in a highly visible place, where you will look at it on a regular basis. For example, when I did this exercise, I made sure I posted it on the door of the 'beer fridge' as I would see it at least twice a day (usually in the evening, although it always depended on how my day was going!).

So, let's not be one of those people who are 'too busy' to work out their 'why', and are simultaneously kissing goodbye to the things they really want out of life. Instead, let's take the approach of a serious property investor by doing the necessary groundwork that will carry us through the tough times and be far more rewarding when we achieve the results we want.

If you haven't yet grasped the reasons why you are doing this, you certainly will by the end of this book. I have adopted the approach that you don't know everything about property investment and are willing to learn new skills and tools in order to re-educate yourself to achieve new results in your life. By adopting this approach, you will be able to craft a way of life that is far beyond your expectations. I have also included, at the end of this book, a worksheet that, if followed, will give you a clear roadmap towards building a successful property portfolio which will feed you and your family for life. For those who, like myself, are a little bit more traditional, who think that writing in a book is one of the most heinous crimes one can commit, then here is a link to a downloadable copy of the worksheet which you can print out and scribe your thoughts on as you work through the book.

www.assafeashouses.com/worksheet

CHAPTER TWO

The Need To Educate Yourself

Having lots of money and going into the world of property investing without knowing what you are doing is a lot like handing a loaded gun to a toddler – sooner or later there is going to be an accident!

Whilst the above statement might seem quite strong, in my experience this is definitely the case. I have met countless people who think they know what it takes to invest in property and who ultimately make a real mess of it because they miss some small detail which ends up costing them thousands of pounds at best. I say 'at best' because as Einstein once famously said: "The difference between genius and stupidity is that genius has its limits!" I was once one of those people who thought: "How hard can it be to make money in property? Surely all you do is buy it, do it up and sell it!" Coming from my estate agency background, I had made tens of thousands of pounds for my clients helping them buy and sell over the course of seven years. However, I quickly learnt there is a *lot* more to property investing than meets the eye.

Those people who know me will know I am a big fan of the phrase, 'You don't know what you don't know', and ultimately it's the things that you don't know that end up taking you out of the game. Many times I have seen rookie investors make a mistake that in isolation would not be considered that bad; however, they have not rectified the mistake (because they don't know how to), or worse, they replicate the mistake several times resulting in missed opportunities or indeed costing them everything they have worked hard for, including their home and family lives if they are not careful.

To illustrate this point, I want to mention Steve and Mark who were classic rookie investors. They were arrogant in their approach, thinking they knew it all and even worse, had friends they were going to learn property investing from (in my experience free advice usually ends up being the most expensive of all). When I met them, they had a portfolio of just three properties and classed themselves as successful 'big time' investors. What they didn't realise (because they didn't know how the numbers work, and their friends didn't either) was that the properties were not working financially so ultimately they were subsidising the lifestyle of their tenants! Not what I would call savvy investing! Trying to explain this to them, however, was really not an option as they simply would not listen. Fine by me gents, I thought, carry on losing money – I'll just buy the properties from you at a discount in the future when you are tired landlords because by then you will be saying: "Property doesn't work". All because they were not humble enough to admit they didn't know it all!

Contrast this with the thousands of other successful investors I know, who are prepared to invest in themselves and learn how to invest in property successfully. Not only are these people humble enough to learn from others who are doing it right, they also follow a success formula which you too can learn. As some of the greatest people who have ever walked this earth will tell you, you need to get educated in your chosen field of expertise and you need to work with people who know what they are doing.

As some level of comfort for you, you should know that not only am I a fully qualified Chartered Surveyor and former estate agent, I have also invested heavily in my personal development over the course of the last eight years. So far, I have invested around £100,000, learning from some of the world's best. 'Is this investment really worth it?' I hear you ask. Well, for me, not only has the return on the investment in myself been substantial, the peace of mind knowing that I am doing things safely is the best thing money can buy! Furthermore, I know that I am protected in my property investing as I have learnt strategies that will work whether the market goes up, down or sideways. This gives huge peace of mind to me and the many other people who have learnt the same strategies and techniques as I have.

At this point, I would like to acknowledge you for being humble enough to read this book as a resource for getting started in property. As much as I would love it to be the best all-encompassing resource around, to put everything there is to know about property investing onto paper would probably amount to a book in excess of 3,500 pages! However, it is more than enough to get you started as a resource and to start building your property business. Whatever the extent of the business you want to build, suffice to say that it will grow as you grow, and making a start with subtle baby steps is definitely the best way to get going. I am sure that many readers of this book will be people who are approaching retirement in the next 10-20 years and want to build security for their future using their pension funds to do so. If you want robustness and longevity in your business, you simply must have a clear strategy and educate yourself well in property investment. This is an on-going process and I am pleased to say that, even after seven years of being engaged in this business, I am still learning.

The word 'strategy' causes a lot of confusion for people in the world of property investing, so it is beneficial to invest some time here understanding what it is. Your strategy is quite simply your approach to property investing. What type of property will you be buying and where? What is the purpose of buying the property, i.e. what will you do with it once you own it? Whilst it might seem that some of these questions are basic, I can assure you this is the starting point to sensible property investment, as understanding your strategy will give you the foundation to your property business. Do this well and your foundation will be solid. Ignore it and you will build your business on a foundation of quicksand, which will fail you at some point in the future – usually when you least expect it. You will also suffer from 'shiny penny' syndrome where you will chase multiple potential property deals without knowing what to do with them or how you will turn them into profit if you acquire them.

What we are going to cover in this book will be the development of a strong foundation in property investing and the strategies of trading properties (buying and selling) as well as buy-to-let (buying and holding). There are many other strategies that you can learn which are beyond the scope of this book. If you learn them, you will have many more tools in your toolbox, which will help you to build your portfolio using little, or none, of your own money. If this sounds inviting to you, then I encourage you to check out the organisation called Tigrent Learning UK Limited, which is where I gained substantial knowledge regarding property investment.

The benefit of attending structured training courses and learning from people who are in the marketplace doing property deals right now cannot be underestimated. I would suggest that you want to learn from people who are 'walking the talk', have a track record in what you want to learn and are doing it all in an ethical manner. I would also suggest that you not only learn the textbook or classroom knowledge, but also get yourself a coach or mentor in the field of property investment who can help you achieve your goals and dreams. Trying to build a property portfolio on your own can be very hard work and you will face a lot of rejection in the process – you need someone professional to guide you and help put you back on your feet when things don't go according to plan.

Depending upon the size of the portfolio you want to create and the timeframe in which you want to create it, I encourage you to learn as much as possible. Deciding on your strategy can be a lot like dating – unless you have been on a few dates with a few people, how do you know what you like and don't like? How do you know what will fit your personality and give you the enjoyment from building your business that you are ultimately seeking? There are many strategies for you to consider, such as:

- Lease options

- Commercial property

- Self-build and renovation

- Higher and better use

- Extensions, alterations and improvements

- Multi-lets, shared housing, student accommodation and HMOs

- Trading properties via auction

- New-build and off-plan development

- Overseas property

I would suggest that you do not invest in the last two on this list unless you are a very experienced investor (100 plus properties in your portfolio), as the potential for being seriously hurt financially is huge.

Each of these strategies will have a certain approach to it, and if you do not follow it correctly, it will end up costing you a lot of money. For example, most rookie investors looking to enter the property investment arena want to start with something glamorous like buying properties abroad. Somehow, owning a property thousands of miles away from us is more appealing than owning a 2-bedroom terraced house in Skegness! However, the legal and financing structure abroad is usually very different from the UK and rookies can end up costing themselves financially by not understanding what they are doing. An example of this is Tom and Whitney who decided to buy property abroad instead of in the UK. They ended up in a frightening situation where they not only lost over £125,000 of their own money, but were also paying five mortgages on properties that hadn't yet been built, purely because of the financing regulations of the countries they were buying in!

I also see many 'uneducated' people falling into the trap of having a little bit of early success in property, which can be devastating in the long run. They are self-taught in a strategy such as buy, do-up and sell. They do this a few times with success and the properties sell well. They then end up in a situation where the latest property won't sell, or the market changes, affecting what they can do with it. Ultimately they are left with a property on which they have to take a substantial loss, or they end up subsidising their tenant's lifestyle over a number of years.

Ultimately, I consider that learning how to invest in property professionally is the safest thing you can do, and it will not only ensure the properties you buy will work, it will also protect your downside should something go wrong and will minimise your stress levels whilst protecting your sanity along the way. To highlight this point, let's refer to Frank and Bob who were successful businessmen I met a few years ago at a networking event. Now to most people these guys were incredibly successful – they had a good business together which was throwing off lots of cash which they then used to buy property. They had built up a portfolio of over 250 units, which in most people's eyes is a huge achievement. However, they were rookies in their approach. They were successful in one area, which was building a business, however they thought they could adopt the same thinking to property investment and do it without the need to educate themselves. Not only were Frank and Bob self-managing their portfolio to save a few pounds, they hadn't done the numbers properly and they didn't realise that their portfolio was actually haemorrhaging cash every single month. This wasn't so much of an issue whilst the property market was going up in the mid-2000s; however, when the market changed in 2008, their business started to slow down and they realised their portfolio was a sinking ship, destined to take everything they had ever worked for from them. This is not the worst situation I have ever seen. I once met a rookie who had a huge portfolio, but again he hadn't focussed on the numbers and was losing over £50,000 a month: he was, as outlined earlier, subsidising his tenants' lifestyle!

Over the last eight years, I have met thousands of successful investors who have recognised the need to get educated first of all, and then gone on to create a financially secure and free future using their knowledge. They have created investment incomes of £2,000 to £10,000 per month, which allows them to live a great lifestyle without the need to rely on a job. Would you like more income than this? That's fine, as long as you are taking action towards your goals rather than talking a great game and doing nothing about it! I know the future is bright for those of you who follow the advice contained within these pages.

In property, it's never about how many properties you own; it's always, always, *always* about how much money the properties you do own put into your pocket at the end of every single month. In summary, educate yourself, get a mentor to support you, learn how to do this properly and you can be sure that your portfolio will feed you well for the rest of your life. Get it wrong and it will eat you alive!

You get what you pay for in this life, and the last thing you want to do is be cheap on investing in yourself. You are the most important asset in your own life!

CHAPTER THREE

Running The Numbers

There is one simple reason why I love property investment so much and that can be summarised in one word. Predictability. The one thing about property is that humans will always need to live somewhere, and ever since we invented the brick, it seems that the building envelope is largely here to stay, at least for our lifetimes. Furthermore, property is the only investment in the world that I am aware of where you can accurately predict your return before you have invested a single penny of your money in it. I guess that's where the saying 'As safe as houses' has come from!

In order for the investment to be predictable, however, you need to ensure you know it works financially. This is easy in theory but so many rookies miss the detail in the numbers which I want to make sure you are fully aware of before you start your investing career. By the end of this chapter you will know what to look for as far as researching the numbers is concerned so that the investment will work for you, as well as knowing some of my top tips on negotiating so you secure yourself a great deal.

Traditionally, most rookies who invest in property buy a property in a good condition or new build/off plan so they don't have to do any work to it. They put down their deposit and then get a buy-to-let mortgage from their high street mortgage broker or bank, and wait to make their money when they sell their property at some point in the future after the market has gone up. They invest for capital appreciation which is great in theory; however, what if the property market doesn't actually go up? This was unthinkable in 2005 and 2006, as the UK market was rising rapidly. Most rookies who were in the market made money from the rising capital values; however, when the market dropped, they lost everything.

So how do we protect ourselves from this happening to us and build a portfolio quickly that will stand the test of time? Well, we start by building it on a solid foundation and not on quicksand! We want to educate ourselves and follow the practical learning contained within the following pages. Always remember that property is a great wealth creation vehicle and the wealthiest people on the planet have largely made their money, or hold their money, in property. Even the greatest actor to have ever lived, Arnold Schwarzenegger, is close to being a billionaire as he has invested heavily in Californian real-estate using his acting commissions. Oprah Winfrey adopts the same approach. If it's good enough for these people, is it good enough for you?

In everything to do with property, the numbers must work in both the acquisition and renovation of the property as well as the running of it should we decide to hold onto it for the long-term. For both of these, follow the templates given within this chapter and you will set yourself up for success. When we buy a property for investment purposes this is when we want to make our money, we are always looking to buy at a discount to the true market value. Contrast this to the rookie who may pay market value for the property (or achieve a small discount), and then hopes to make money in the future.

Buying at a discount is important for a number of reasons:

i.   Regardless of the purchase price, we will still get the same rental income for a property where there is evidence of similar properties achieving the same rent.

ii. The lower the purchase price, the lower our monthly mortgage payments, which will bring in a comparatively higher monthly income from each unit we acquire.

iii. In line with (ii) above, we will also require less deposit money to go into each property and therefore we can buy more properties with the money we have available to us.

iv. As we have bought at a discount, the possibility of 'recycling' our original deposit out of the property and into another property becomes a lot higher. (If this point appears confusing and you don't understand it now, you will by the end of this chapter.)

v. By buying right, we can always sell the property quickly for its true market value and make our money then (trading properties).

We are ultimately aiming to buy the property at a discount of at least 25%-30% below what it is actually worth on the open market. Whilst some of you may be thinking this is impossible, I can assure that it is possible if you are prepared to put the time and effort into this business. In short, it comes down to a numbers game of making lots of offers on lots of different properties to make sure you are buying at a discount to the true market value.

At this point, I must confess to you that you won't be buying detached, modern, executive-style homes if you want to build a successful property portfolio as, ultimately, the numbers on these properties don't work. However, don't take my word for it – learn the templates I teach you and then you can feel free to run the numbers on these types of properties and see what the end result is. What we are looking for are the types of properties that are typically in high demand in most areas of the UK. These tend to be 2- and 3-bedroom semi-detached and terraced homes. We also want properties that will provide us with a regular monthly income and therefore we will be looking for properties that are typically under £100,000 in value.

You will no doubt have noticed that we have here our first two benchmarks in property investing: the type of property we are looking for and the ceiling value for the investment itself. This will also give us a clue to the location in the country we are going to have to search within in order to find the right property. This might involve some travelling in order to get to know the investment area well, however it is well worth it, as the long-term benefits will not be found in any other investment vehicle in my experience.

Whilst we are on that point, I would say this: a lot of rookies I meet want someone else to do the work for them so they don't have to. Whilst leveraging your time may seem like a wise thing to do, always bear in mind that no-one will look after your money and your investment like you will, so I encourage you to learn this process well and do it yourself (at least initially) so you know what you are looking for. Should you then decide to find someone else to do it, you can be sure that the investment works because you have the knowledge to double-check it for yourself. You will also appreciate what is involved within the service you are paying for.

To highlight this point, I want to mention Dave who was a computer technician earning a substantial amount of money fixing people's IT problems. He made a decision to start investing in property but, he claimed, he didn't have the time to do it himself. So he paid someone else a small fortune to find the properties, renovate them and find tenants for him. Over the course of two years he bought five properties from these people; however, the renovation works were poorly done, resulting in properties that were frequently empty because of their condition and huge void periods eating into his monthly income. He didn't realise this, as his income from his job was so good; however, when the recession came and he lost his job, those five properties ended up costing him almost everything he had.

Let's protect ourselves by taking a look at the monthly cash flow formula we will be using to check to see if our proposed deals work. What we are looking for is to ensure that the property we are buying provides us with a monthly investment income in our pocket once all the expenses are covered. Most rookies think that the only expense is the monthly mortgage as they usually self-manage the property; however, what about wear and tear, maintenance, voids and covering things that go wrong during the tenants' time in the property? We need to make allowances for these in our figures otherwise we will end up shooting ourselves in the financial foot and we will be working to support the portfolio, rather than having the portfolio support us each month.

What does this look like in practice? Well, we are all aware that we are going to have a mortgage on the investment property if we are building our portfolio in an efficient manner. Buying properties outright for cash is fine if you want to limit yourself to owning a few properties and you are lucky enough to have a big pot of money when you are starting out, but in my experience this only applies to a minority of people. Therefore, we want to use financial leverage via the use of a mortgage which will allow us to borrow around 75% of the purchase price of the property. For the purposes of our calculations and to ensure the deals work for the long-term, we want to employ an interest rate on our mortgages of 6%. Whilst it is true that you can get mortgages at a cheaper rate than this, it is likely that interest rates will only go one way in the future, and you want to make sure you are hedging yourself against interest rate rises in the future which will seriously harm your investment income if you have not made allowances for this.

The next expense we will have is the fee to cover the management of the property on a monthly basis, as you will need the services of a good-quality letting agent to manage the property for you, especially if you want a hassle-free life! HMRC currently allow you to tax deduct 15% of your monthly income from the property for the employment of a specialist letting agent in the management of your property, so we will use this figure for our calculations. Here's a great tip for you: even if your letting agent only charges you 8% per month to manage the property, you will also need to manage the letting agent, and therefore you may as well pay yourself the remaining 7% per month for doing so!

We then need to build into our calculations a wear-and-tear allowance for running the properties on a monthly basis. (This is the one area that almost all rookie investors completely miss and as such find themselves in a financial hole when the tenant rings up on December 22nd saying that their boiler has blown up! For some reason this always happens around Christmas time!) At the time of writing, HMRC will allow you to deduct 10% of the gross rent receivable as a wear-and-tear allowance for furnished lettings, so this will be a good rule of thumb to use. If you are furnishing your properties for rent, which will depend on the market you are aiming for, it would seem good practice to do so based on what HMRC allow us to do as investors. The wear-and-tear budget is an amount of money that we will set aside in a separate bank account every single month in order to ensure we are covered should a kitchen or bathroom or boiler need to be replaced at the end of, or during the course of, a tenancy agreement.

Finally, I want you to factor in a contingency to your calculations of an additional 5% of the monthly income so that you know you are safe and you are hedging yourself against the unforeseen. Too many times I have seen rookie investors running their portfolios too tightly and taking too much money out of the business too soon, which ultimately means it fails at some point. What's true in business is true in property and I cannot emphasise enough the need to nurture and grow your portfolio in a safe manner so it feeds you for the long-term rather than becoming a financial noose around your neck.

What does this look like in practice? Let's take a look at the following example for illustration purposes.

Property type: 3-bedroom terrace with a market value of £100,000.

Market Rent: £650 per calendar month.

From this information, we can work out the likely return from this property:

Monthly Rental Income	£650.00
Mortgage costs per month	£375.00
£100,000 x 75% =	£75,000
£75,000 x 6% =	£4,500
£4,500 divided by 12 =	£375
Lettings Fee @ 15% of rent =	£97.50
Wear and Tear Allowance @ 10% of rent =	£65.00
Contingency @ 5% of rent =	£32.50
Total Investment Income	£80 per calendar month

For those of you who are worried about getting the maths right on this, I can assure you that this is all that you need to master, and once you have practiced this by following the above template enough times, you will be in the strong position where you know just by looking at the properties and the likely rent they will produce whether they are worth investing in or not.

Looking at the above example, you might be thinking that it's not worth investing in the property for an income of only £80 per month; however, let's get some further perspective on this. This is a monthly income that comes in regardless of whether you go to work or not. Over time, it is likely to grow naturally with inflation or as you pay down the mortgage, should you decide to go down the route of a repayment mortgage. However, you will also have bought the property at a discount, which is likely to mean that you have around £25,000 worth of equity in the property (equity, as taught to me by the 'Real Rich Dad' from the book *Rich Dad Poor Dad*, is the difference between what you own and what you owe).

Furthermore, it's an investment income that you can pass on to your children. If you build your business in the right manner, you may not have to pay much tax (speak to a good tax advisor, not an accountant!) on this, as there are legitimate ways to do this through the running and growth of your property business. Think about how much work you would have to do in your current job in order to generate that sort of income every single month for the rest of your life! I say the rest of your life because, when you get this right, you will end up in a situation where the tenants that occupy your properties will do so for a very long time and will pay their rent on time and in full every single month.

Make sure you are getting the best return on the time that you spend on your property business and learn to leverage the use of other people in your business. Your three skills as someone who is serious in this business are (1) to educate yourself as much as possible about property investment strategies and techniques so you can run this business safely, (2) to find property deals, and (3) to find the finance to acquire them. All the rest of the buying, renovating, selling and renting of properties you will leave to someone else as your time is far too valuable to be consumed with 'saving' £90-£100 per month per property by managing them yourself.

As a point of reference, I met a rookie called Shane at a networking event and was gobsmacked by his response to my innocent question: "Did you have a good weekend?" Shane proceeded to tell me all about the fact that he had spent his entire two-day weekend changing a toilet cistern at a property he owned that he was renting out. His attitude towards tenants was damning to say the least, and I had to wonder why he was getting his hands dirty doing this work when a competent plumber would have probably been able to do the same job in about an hour. You have to ask yourself the same question – are two days away from your family or friends worth the 'saving' that doing a job like this on your own would produce? To my mind, it's a no-brainer as you more than likely want to get into property in order to have more free time.

The worst offenders are definitely those people who have some element of skill in DIY, or renovating properties forms part of their day job. I met two rookies called Gerald and Mark who thought they knew it all and were going into property with the same limited knowledge I once had, thinking: 'How hard can it really be?' They told me that they were living in Brighton and were renovating a property in the West Midlands that they had allegedly 'bought cheap at auction'. That weekend, they were due to drive from Brighton to Hull to remove a kitchen from a property they had bought on eBay and then drive back down to the West Midlands to fit it! In reality, they had paid market value for the property (it seemed cheap to them because a comparable property in Brighton would have been much more expensive), and then spent two days of their lives driving around the country fitting a second-hand kitchen into a property with all the associated headaches that come with it. Despite my best efforts, they were adamant that their approach was right – you just can't help some people who cannot see past the end of their noses! I urge you not to be one of those people!

Doing The Research

How do we do the research on each property we are interested in buying so that we acquire a property that feeds us rather than one that eats us? Let's take a step-by-step look at that so we can be sure that we are protecting ourselves in a major way. The first steps of research can all be done from the comfort of our own home with a computer and Internet connection. Most people have heard of the website Rightmove.co.uk so we shall use this as our research tool to get started.

Step One: Open your internet browser (you might want to download Mozilla Firefox for your property research, as there is a very smart tool we can use as part of our research which we will come on to later (called PropertyBee). Open two tabs on your browser, both with Rightmove on them.

Step Two: On the first tab, go into Rightmove 'For Sale' and search for 3 bedroom terraced properties up to a maximum of £100,000. You will want to consider towns and areas of cities (not cities themselves as you will be overwhelmed with the number of properties that come up in your search) that are in the North of England (North of Birmingham) and South Wales as sensible areas for investment. At this stage, I am going to caution you against investing in the Welsh Valleys as invariably you will end up with lots of headaches rather than properties that work for you. This is because these areas are predominantly rental areas rather than home owner areas. Whilst this may seem ideal to buy properties to rent out here, the downside is you will only be able to sell it onto another investor who will want to buy at a discount. This could mean you losing money if you need to sell quickly.

Step Three: Your search results should yield at least 65 properties for sale otherwise you need to pick a different area.

Step Four: Pick five properties at random from the selection that has come up in your search results. At this stage, we are not worried about whether or not they require work; as long as they are 3 bedroom terraced properties in a particular town, then that is ok.

Step Five: Now go to the second tab in your web browser and look at Rightmove 'To Rent' in the same area that you searched for properties 'For Sale' in. Search for the same property type, but do not put a limit on the rental figures.

Then, once you have the search results in front of you, use the map function to narrow in on a property which is comparable to the one you have found which is for sale. This will give you a good idea of the likely rental figure for the property you are looking at.

Step Six: Repeat Step Five for the five properties you have identified for sale and then use the rental figures to run the investment calculation we reviewed earlier. I would encourage you to work out each and every calculation on a separate sheet of A4 paper by hand, rather than setting up an Excel spreadsheet, for the simple reason that if you make a mistake in your formula setting up the spreadsheet, then you will replicate the mistake several times over! I have seen this happen many times and it's not pretty!

Step Seven: Once you have worked out your five investment calculations for the first area you have chosen, you then want to choose another nine towns or areas of cities in the UK to explore and do the same exercise with these, so that you will have done 50 investment calculations in total. Do not shortcut this step as you could miss an incredible investment area and not even know it.

Step Eight: Review the 10 areas and you will see that three of those areas will work better than the other seven. Therefore, discard the seven and focus on the three areas where you can consider investing once you have been to visit them and see if they are the kind of areas you want to buy properties in.

Step Nine: Once you have the three proposed areas that work on a strictly numbers basis, you will then need to plan to visit them all in turn so that you can understand exactly what is going on in the area as whole and if it will suit your investment needs. My suggestion would be to visit on three weekends in quick succession and take a good drive around the areas to see if they feel right to you. I always imagine someone close to me when I am driving around the areas and I ask myself the question: "Would I be happy to let them live there?" If the answer is no, then I would move on to the next area.

Step Ten: Once you have visited the three areas, you will have a very good idea about which one you will want to invest in. Your task is to then visit your investment area at least once a month to continue to build up your local knowledge and become the local expert on residential property investment in your area.

This 10-step process helps you narrow down the entirety of the UK to find your investment area. Once you have done this, you can spend some time with the letting agents in the area asking them what properties are in demand and in what areas, so that you know you are buying properties which have demand rather than buying for the sake of owning a property and then wondering what you are going to do with it! By owning properties in high-demand areas, you will ensure you have minimal void periods and your tenants will always look after the property they are living in.

Negotiating The Deal

As I have already mentioned, we are looking to acquire properties at a discount compared to their true market value so we can make our money when we buy whilst giving ourselves the best possible chance of recycling our original deposit out of the property into another deal in the future.

This is stacking the odds massively in our favour that the deal will work, and it is also a hedge against any possible drops in house prices in the future as we have already bought the property well, so the possibility of ending up in a negative equity situation (where the mortgage is more than the property value) is greatly reduced.

In my experience, most people who are entering the arena of residential property investment do not fully understand the process of negotiation, and I hear of some horrendous mistakes being made by rookie investors trying to buy property. Here's what I will say: buying properties is a big commitment, and all too often it's easy to get talked up into paying the asking price for the property by a smooth-talking estate agent rather than working hard to get yourself a good deal.

What I must tell you is that you will face a lot of rejection from homeowners and estate agents if you are going to buy properties in the right manner and acquire them at a discount. Not everyone is going to accept an offer 30% less than what the property is worth; that said, how many people do you realistically need to accept your offers in order to make this worthwhile for you? Would 20-30 people accepting your offers make this a worthwhile venture for you? I would point out that you will make a lot of money and build a solid portfolio if you get this many people accepting your below-market-value offers over the course of the next 2-3 years.

Here are some of my top tips on negotiating deals so that you can be readily armed in making offers to clients and estate agents as you go about building your business:

DON'T:

- Ask the seller or estate agent what the lowest price is they will accept! The answer is always the asking price!

- Get emotionally attached to the deal or the seller's situation – this is a sure-fire way to overpay for the property.

- Appear desperate to get the property – there will always, always be another property deal that will come along if you are prepared to work for it.

- Try to bully people into taking your offer or manipulate a painful situation for a seller to your advantage – this is a big no-no in my book. I am a great believer in what goes around comes around and at some point in the future it will come back to haunt you.

- Be too hasty to get an offer accepted, or chase a property at auction by a few hundred or few thousand pounds. You will almost always regret it in the future. My best advice is to set your maximum bid price for the property and then stick to this limit regardless of what happens.

DO:

- Be empathetic with a seller's situation and do all that you can to help them out where possible – as long as this does not mean overpaying for the property or jeopardising yourself financially.

- Educate yourself in different property investment techniques so that you can help more people with creative offers on their properties to enable you to purchase them. For instance, you will be able to make two or three different offers on properties, when you know what you are doing, such as (1) a cash offer now; (2) part cash now, part cash later; (3) a longer-term agreement under a form of lease option where you agree to pay the seller a monthly amount of money and then buy their property from them at some point in the future.

- Make lots and lots of offers on properties that meet your criteria for buying and that fit your strategy. I will venture to say that you need to have at least 25 offers out at any one time in order to be in with the best chances of securing a great deal.

- Follow up on your offers every single month at least. Whilst you may get a 'no' initially, this is not 'no' forever, it's just 'no' now! If you continually follow up on the offer (without harassing the seller) then you will stand a much better chance of getting it accepted.

- Use thought-provoking questions in your negotiations such as: *"How close can you come to £x?" "How soon do you want to sell the property?" "What are you going to do once you have sold the property?"*

- Always have a cup of tea with the seller of a property wherever possible (the Great British Empire was built on cups of tea!), and talk to them as human beings rather than trying to buy their property from them without getting to know them first. People will sell to people they like, so make sure the seller likes you as a person before you start talking about buying the property from them at a discounted price.

Many people I meet who want to get into property investing have not had much experience at negotiating, so I have a fun game for you to play which will help hone your skills and turn you into a negotiating ninja! Here's the game for those of you who are ready to play it – you have to go out into the big, wide world and get something for free. Now this can be anything from a free paperclip to a free cup of coffee or something of much greater value, but the value of the item is not important here. What is important is the fact that you have gone out to ask for it and got what you asked for. It's all about taking the small wins along the way which will help you to build your skills and confidence as well as the powerful questions that you will ask people to help you in your quest to get something for free.

Here are the rules to the game that you must abide by: you are not allowed to steal or cheat someone out of the item and it has to be something that comes from a genuine interaction with other people. It also cannot be something like going around to your friend's or parents' house for dinner and claiming that you got a free meal! The reason I am suggesting that you do this is because the more you do it with people on a regular basis, the better you will be at negotiating and hence the better chance you will have of getting your offers accepted.

In order to illustrate how much fun this game can be I want to walk you through an example that happened to my partner and me at a service station, driving back home late one night. We stopped to grab a coffee, and the interaction with the service staff helped us to walk away with a free packet of biscuits whilst making friends with the staff behind the counter, who were left feeling happy and cheerful from our interaction! We initially approached the counter and gave a high-five to the girl taking our order. Immediately she looked a little confused and was taken aback when I asked with a cheery smile: "How are you?" Now, many people in the service industry do not get asked this question and, after an exchange of pleasantries, I also asked her if she was having a good day. I took a genuine interest in her as a person and recall making some joke about the last thing she needed was some nutter like me turning up to make her day extra special! I then placed my order, and after she asked if I would like anything else, I remarked,: "Yes, I would like something complimentary please!"

Now, I won't mention the particular coffee chain, but suffice to say that I have tried these negotiation tactics probably 30 times at various stores and got nowhere! One lesson you can take from this example is to never give up (famous words from Winston Churchill), so I tried and tried and tried to get something for free from this particular coffee stand. I faced plenty of rejection, but still did not give up. When I noticed a packet of shortbread in a display stand which had a broken biscuit in it, I casually remarked that *they couldn't sell them because they were broken!* We all laughed due to my persistence and collected our coffees ready to leave. I high-fived the staff and told them that they were angels and to have a great evening, and as we turned to leave, one of the staff picked up the broken shortbread biscuits and said: "Here, you can take these with you!" I was actually a little taken aback and checked to make sure that she was being sincere, before leaving, pleased as punch, with my coffee and free packet of shortbread biscuits! This might not sound like the biggest win in the world, but trust me when I say that every little helps when you are honing your negotiation skills. Be light-hearted and likeable and you will win the day and make a friend in the process, whilst making a positive impact on someone's day.

You could, of course, choose not to play this game and not participate in any of the other exercises in this book. Most people choose not to, and they fool themselves into thinking that they will do it when they have a great deal in front of them. The reality is, though, that they fall into the 'rookie' category and go out and make horrendous mistakes, which they then spend the rest of their lives paying for. Or they effectively kiss goodbye to their goals and dreams, as they aren't prepared to do the work necessary to get them. I know that's not you, however, otherwise you wouldn't be reading this book! So, I encourage you to put the book down now and go out and negotiate something for free to get that win, which will build up your confidence and help you believe that you will make this whole property thing happen.

CHAPTER FOUR

Finding Deals

Finding deals is easy, right? You just go to the estate agents and make them an offer, right? Or wave at an auctioneer for a few minutes until they bang their gavel on the rostrum?! Welcome to the number one rookie mistake that people make who want to get into property investing. Whilst it is true that estate agents sell properties, they are unlikely to be your friends when it comes to buying properties as an investor. They do not understand your business and how it works because, if they did, they would be property investors themselves and not estate agents! I know this as I used to be an estate agent, and I kick myself when I look back at all the great deals that passed through my hands making countless thousands for my then clients! In my experience, most estate agents don't take too kindly to investors making offers that are well below what the property is on the market for and most agents can be unrealistic in the figures they ask for properties that they have for sale. In short, you have a situation that can create a lot of friction between people's egos and may result in you not getting the deals you want. As a former estate agent, I can assure you that they often have big egos, which can be easily bruised. Thankfully I have got rid of my ego now that I am a professional property investor…

So, how do we find deals and stand the best possible chances of success? Well, the short answer to that is there are quite possibly hundreds of different ways to find property deals that most people do not even think about, and as a result they miss the best deals out there. Your best deals will come from negotiating directly with the seller of the properties themselves rather than via any third party agent or representative. They will also come about as a result of your continued persistence in following up each and every offer you make time and time again, until the property has been physically sold to someone else or you buy it.

As a basic minimum, you should be following up each offer you make at least once a month. If you have 25 offers placed on properties, then you will need to set aside around 4-5 hours per month to follow up these offers. Why is this so important? Well, as one of my mentors suggests: *"The money is in the database"* and he is absolutely right. Most of the successful property investors that I speak to are buying properties now that they first offered on some 6-24 months ago. Indeed, I have followed up properties myself for between 1-2 years and have ended up buying some cracking deals that no-one else has managed to secure because they are approaching it in a rookie manner and not sticking to this hard and fast rule of persistently following up their offers time and again.

To explain further what I mean, I once met a father and son partnership, Rick and Simon, who were classic rookie investors. The one big problem these guys had is they had struck a deal with Rick's brother who happened to have a lot of money, which he was prepared to lend to Rick and Simon so they could start their property investment career. This one small element of success in finding a pot of money literally turned them into 'starving men at a buffet' where they went out buying properties left, right and centre. Whilst most people will think there is nothing wrong with this, the main issue was they felt that they didn't need to educate themselves in how to buy property, as they were already 'investing' and they were achieving a 6%-10% discount from the price estate agents were asking for the properties. Unfortunately for them, when I met them in 2007, their buying frenzy was running rife literally just before the market crashed. I haven't seen them since, however I can guess what has happened to them. They lost a fortune and their family relationships have more than likely been ruined.

On the other side of the coin are Adrian and Clare, who are expert investors in every sense of the word. Not only do they secure some amazing property deals 30%-50% below the market value, they also help a tremendous number of people. This is something to take note of because, when they first meet someone who is looking to sell their property, their primary aim is to help the owner find a way to sell it other than selling it to them! This might seem like backwards logic, however it positions them in the mind of the seller as their friend who is willing to help them. If the seller does all the things that Adrian and Clare suggest to sell their property and it doesn't work, they offer the seller an exit from the property at their offer price. What's interesting to note from my perspective is the frequency they get their offers accepted and also how many sellers refer their friends to Adrian and Clare. Something to think about! I mentioned it before: what goes around comes around, and this is so true in the world of property investing.

There are some more rules to playing the investing game that I want you to have in mind when you are going out making your offers on properties, and these are as follows:

1. **Stand in your integrity.** This means doing what you say you are going to do. If you say you are going to buy someone's property, *you do it!* It's really not fair to say that you are going to buy someone's house from them if they are going through repossession, for example, and then pull out of the deal later on. If you are unsure about any aspects of buying the property, then do not shake hands on a deal until you have the detail finalised. It will only come back to haunt you later on!

2. **No 'low-balling' the price at exchange of contracts.** Some rookie investors agree a price on a property and string the sellers along right up to exchange of contracts to only then put in a lower offer and demand that the sellers accept it otherwise they will pull out of the deal. This is unethical at best and, again, you can expect this one to revisit you at some point in the future if you try it.

3. **Do not take advantage of people who are in distress.** This is an absolute no-no. Help them out as much as you can using your moral compass to guide you and help them find a solution to their problems. This does not mean that you just give them money to keep them in the house or fall for a sob story. It does mean that you put their needs first and yours second. You can still make them an offer that works for you after you have given them a number of other options; if they accept it, that is up to them.

4. **Exchange contracts quickly.** Once you have agreed the deal, proceed as quickly as possible to exchange of contracts so the sellers know they have a solid deal. Rookies will drag out a deal while they pull the finance together and this is a big mistake, as invariably it will cause friction somewhere along the way and they will lose the deal. You should already have some element of finance in place to buy the deal before you agree it otherwise you are setting yourself up for a fall.

5. **Do not spread yourself too thinly.** If you have a few properties being renovated at the same time, this may cause you some cash flow problems, which we will look at later on when it comes to renovating the properties. This may cause you to break your commitments with people from whom you have agreed to buy properties. It's no excuse – deal with each property as an individual case and move onto the next.

Now that you have a clear understanding of how we are approaching the investing game, let's take a look at where some of these phenomenal deals may be lurking so you have the best chance of securing some great property purchases.

Finding the deals

There are many places where property deals can be found, and whilst the following list is not exhaustive, it will certainly give you a good head start on where to look and how to go about finding them. Let's look at my top-ten selection of areas to find deals:

- **Your database.** Most of your deals will be found here and it's such an obvious place to look that most people overlook it! They spend a lot of time going out, viewing properties and making offers, and then they forget about them and let all their hard work slip between their fingertips. Every offer you make must be recorded in a database and then followed up on a regular basis in order to ensure you have the best possible chance of it being accepted.

- **Letting agents.** Whilst most rookies deal through estate agents, the smart investors know that letting agents also deal in property and will know that a certain number of their clients will be looking to sell their properties over time. If you offer to leave the property with them to manage once you buy it, they will more than likely arrange an introduction to the property owner.

- **Private adverts in the newspaper.** Rookie landlords and sellers will try and save money on agents' fees and advertise properties themselves in the newspaper for sale and to let. Call these people and see if they are open to selling their properties. You never know where it can lead! You can also place your own advert in the newspaper, telling people that you want to buy their property, which may generate calls from people who want to sell but don't want to use estate agents.

- **Leaflet Drops.** Use these to target an area where you want to buy properties and make sure you are distributing leaflets accurately to the doors in the area at least every other month. Be sensible and selective over where you are leafleting. Whilst it may sound great leafleting 100,000 properties, the costs of doing this on a regular basis may be unsustainable, and it's unlikely that you will get better results than targeting an area of 10,000 homes 10 times in a year.

- **Auctions.** These can be great places to find spectacular deals, however you must make sure that you have carried out all your due diligence on the property before you attend the auction. If you have never attended an auction before, you need to be aware that the moment the hammer falls, you have exchanged contracts on the property (assuming you are the winning bidder) and you are legally bound to buy the property. Whilst auctions hold a higher proportion of really good deals, it's also fair to say they are the one place where those properties which may be a little quirky or have a dodgy legal title are also sold, so you need to make sure your solicitor has checked over the legal pack before you make a bid. You also need to be aware of something called 'the modern method of auction' which has become very fashionable with some estate agents. I am really against this method of sale as effectively, when you win the auction, it is just for the right to buy the property within a certain timescale. My objection to this comes down to the delays that people invariably encounter in the purchase process and many people I have spoken to lose thousands of pounds in the form of reservation fees passed onto the agents who have wrongfully, in my view, kept this money in an unethical manner. My best advice here is to always read the small print and look at what you are getting into before you try and buy a property via this method.

- **Owners selling properties themselves.** The recession has created a market for people trying to sell their property themselves without paying an agent a fee for doing so. These properties are easy to identify as they usually have a hand-painted 'For Sale' sign outside or, even worse, a piece of paper stuck to the upstairs bedroom window with 'For Sale' written in pencil! These can be a great source of deals; however, make sure you are treating the sellers with respect as many of them won't be trained in the art of negotiation or house buying and selling; therefore they will need some guidance from you as to what is involved and how quickly they can expect to move. Look after them and they will look after you.

- **Estate agents.** Some estate agents can be really good to you as an investor, however finding them takes work as most will dismiss your offers and consider you to be a waste of their time rather than someone who can buy the properties from them that they cannot sell. My guidance here is to spend some time talking to all of them and test them out with a few offers and see what happens. If the feedback is not positive, do not spend time bashing your head against a wall! Move on as there are plenty more avenues to find deals.

- **Websites.** I am sure you will be familiar with such websites as Rightmove and Zoopla for finding property investment deals; however, there are certainly other avenues you can explore such as 'for sale by owner' websites and even eBay! Get creative about this, as the Internet is a great search tool for you to start to really get to know your area and find some great deals. However, it is only one research tool and will not substitute getting into the area and doing the groundwork to find the best deals.

- **Talking to people.** One of my mentors is a huge fan of talking to people all the time. He talks to everyone and makes sure they leave with a business card which lets them know he buys houses. He will talk to everyone in an area whether he meets them in the local shop, a property networking event or indeed the local pub. I encourage you to do the same, as you never know where it will lead. The good thing about the Great British Public is that everyone loves to talk about property and you may well get a lead to one of their friends who is looking to sell their property quickly and as such will accept a good offer on it.

- **Property networking events.** Usually your chosen area of investment will have a property networking event and I encourage you to attend, as you never know who you might meet. There will usually be (rookie) landlords in attendance who may be looking to sell some or all of their properties. Or you may meet someone who later transpires to be a Joint Venture partner and you can start to do some deals together. Either way, you will be glad you attended!

If you make a conscious effort to keep working through the above list each and every month, you are almost guaranteed to find some great deals! Assuming you are pleasant, polite and helpful in your approach to talking to sellers of property, you will be able to place an offer with them 25%+ below market value and still part company as friends. This will lead to you building up your database of 25+ offers on properties at any one time and by doing so, if you continue to follow up on them, you will secure a great deal. It might seem like a lot of work, but each and every deal that you do will net you around £15,000+ in equity which could be realised if you sell the property on the open market, just for buying it right in the first place. My question to you here would be: how hard would you have to work in your current job or business in order to generate the same level of cash? For most people in the UK, this is equivalent to six months net salary, so it's well worth putting the time and effort into finding these deals. My view is, do the work quickly and enjoy the benefits for longer.

Once you have found the property, the next question I usually get asked is: *"How do you put the finance together for it?"* Well, it's a good job that you asked this question, as that is the subject of the next chapter! Let's turn the page to keep learning about how we can finance all these great deals with limited resources.

CHAPTER FIVE

Finding Money

Before we get into the main crux of finding finance for your great property deals, there is an important principle we must explore in order to be truly successful as a residential property investor. This is the principle of buying a property below market value. Why is this so important? Primarily, your ability to buy properties right will affect your progress in building the foundation level of your portfolio so there is 'safety in numbers' in the development of your business. By buying right, we put ourselves in a position where we can potentially draw out our initial deposit at a later date so that we can then recycle this money onto another property deal, allowing us to buy several properties with one investment pot rather than just leaving our money in one property which is what the rookies in the investment world do because they don't know any different.

To give you an example, let's look at Billy, who is a rookie investor who happens to earn quite a lot of money from his day job. Billy has a lot of excess income, which he had been previously stockpiling in a bank account, but he realised that this was not giving him a great return. So, after watching Sarah Beeney on television, Billy went to the local estate agent and bought a property that needed some work and he could renovate in his spare time and then rent it out.

Now, here are some crucial errors that Billy made which are well worth noting. As Billy chose to buy the property via an estate agent, he actually ended up in a position where he over-paid for the property in its current condition and underestimated the cost of renovation, as he was not skilled in the art of renovation at all. He paid £80,000 for a property which was worth £100,000 in good condition, thinking that he had a good deal. It took Billy over six months to renovate the property in his spare time of evenings and weekends, and because he didn't understand how surveys work (something that we will cover later), he ended up missing several items of crucial work on the property when he looked at it initially and this cost him an extra £7,000 on top his original refurbishment budget of £15,000.

By the time all the fees for the buying of the property had been taken into account, because he used his family solicitor to buy it for him and also used his 'friend' who worked for a bank to sort out his 65% loan to value mortgage, Billy was in a position where he was locked into a 5-year fixed rate mortgage product (he didn't know at that time whether he was going to keep the property, refinance it or sell it on, however the 5-year fixed rate deal that his mortgage advisor friend had arranged ensured his friend made quite a lot of money from Billy). His total spend, including renovation costs, was in excess of £25,000. When added to the purchase price of the property of £80,000, this meant his total investment was £105,000 for a property that was worth £100,000! Now, this may seem to be ok as at least he has the property to show for his efforts, right? Well, let's take a deeper look at this situation to find out the true impact of what has happened to Billy.

As Billy received a 65% loan to value mortgage from the mortgage company, they lent him just £52,000, which meant that Billy had to invest £28,000 of his own money in the property in the form of a deposit. Remember that the mortgage was fixed for 5 years, which means that Billy is now locked into owning the property and keeping that same finance on the property or else he will have to pay a redemption penalty of 5% should he choose to pay back the loan earlier through either refinancing or selling the property. This means that any potential profit Billy might make from renovating and selling the property would be eaten up by the redemption penalty of £2,600.

Not only this, but the opportunity cost to Billy by taking six months to renovate the property part-time is that he is the one paying the monthly mortgage payments of £260 (interest rate at 6%) which adds another £1,560 to his costs. Plus, he loses the possibility of receiving rental income from the property at £500 per month (had he bought in a different area with higher demand, he would have been able to add another £100 per month to his monthly rental income), which is around £2,500 of lost rental income.

Let's also look at the impact on Billy's personal financial situation from doing this deal. He needs to find the initial £28,000 in deposit funds to buy the property, but he also needs to put another £25,000 into the deal to cover things like renovation costs and fees, bringing Billy's total financial exposure to the deal to £53,000. This is money that is locked into the property and cannot be recycled onto another deal as he is on a fixed rate deal for 5 years. He has also spent more money on the property than it is worth meaning he has over-capitalised on the purchase – not a good position to be in!

Even if Billy did take the redemption hit of £2,600 plus fees to refinance the property away from the current mortgage company onto another lender, the maximum loan to value that he could achieve would be 75% based on the market value of the property which would be £100,000 not the £105,000 that he has spent in total. This would mean that he can achieve a 75% mortgage on the property (£75,000) which would release £75,000 minus the £52,000 original mortgage = £23,000 minus fees of approximately £2,500, so Billy would walk away with around £20,500 to invest into another property. By choosing the wrong financing option and not knowing about all the available mortgage products on the open market, it seems that this alone has cost Billy £5,000 plus in fees. I don't know many people who can afford to take a £5,000 loss and enjoy the experience!

Furthermore, he would have increased his total spend on the property to around £107,500 whilst the property is still only worth £100,000 so, in reality, he has over-capitalised by £7,500. His own funds of £32,500 will remain locked into the property forever. Some people will argue that he can pull his money out of the deal when the property has gone up in value, but again this is rookie thinking. I personally do not advise people to think about refinancing the property more than once after the initial purchase and that should be to get back all of your initial investment. If you don't get back your initial investment, frankly you should have bought better or be comfortable with leaving money in the deal.

If it seems that the above scenario is a catalogue of errors and somewhat unlikely, then I can tell you that, in my experience, every rookie investor that I speak to and enquire how they are buying properties will be doing this or a variation of this. I cannot emphasise enough the true value of quality education in the field of property investing so that you know what you are doing and you are *protecting the downside*, as Richard Branson would say. The worst rookie mistake I see people make is to do something similar to the above, and then think that they know how property investing works! They then go around to their friends and family explaining to them what an expert they are on property and encourage them to invest with them, doing deals which frankly do not work and will end up costing everyone involved a lot of money. It is absolutely horrible to witness people making these sorts of errors and watching them sink themselves and their family at the same time. I know this because I have had to coach people out of these sorts of situations in the past, and it's quite an unpleasant experience telling someone that they are potentially facing bankruptcy unless we take some extreme action to prevent it.

So, how do we buy right and protect the downside in the same process? Well, let's look at Debbie's situation now.

Debbie is a true professional investor in every sense of the word and, interestingly, she did something that most people will not do which is ultimately why she is so successful. Debbie chose to first look at herself and understand her limitations as far as her knowledge of property investing was concerned. When she started her journey in property, she had very little experience; in fact, she was a tenant. She chose to enter a fairly male-dominated field, and make an investment in herself and her education first so she knew how to work with property properly. The sum of money that Debbie invested in herself was significant, and most people who know what she invested in herself and her education think that she was crazy; she could have bought a property with the same money as it was equivalent to a deposit. I, however, know otherwise, as she is a smart lady.

Once Debbie had the education and corresponding support network around her, she was able to confidently go out into the market place using a lot of the techniques we have covered in this book so far, and place multiple offers on properties, building a robust database that she continued to visit time and again in order to find some amazing property deals. Not only did she start doing deals like a professional, she put herself in line to do many deals using other people's money.

How does that work? I hear you ask. It's pretty simple really when you know how. Well, the theory is! Doing it in practice takes time and courage to do it right, as well as a strong element of accountability to put you in the right place at the right time to get the deals that no-one else does.

What Debbie does differently to rookie investors is that she is able to make her money when she buys, by buying properties at a discount to the true market value. This allows her to recycle her money time and again onto more and more property deals. Let's talk through one of her recent deals that she did using none of her money. Debbie found a property in her local investment area using many of the creative techniques we talked about earlier for finding great deals. She made plenty of offers, and after eight months one deal in particular started to gain momentum. She had offered £58,350 on a property that needed approximately £12,000 spending on it including fees. This brought her total investment up to £70,350 on a property that was worth around £105,000 on the open market. She obtained the right finance on it initially, which allowed her the flexibility to choose whether to sell the property when it was renovated to a good condition, or refinance it to cash out her deposit and roll it into another deal. This is a classic professional investor trait: working on two exits from a deal whilst also buying right to create value and make money when you buy.

Debbie chose to raise the money from a family member whom she would pay an interest rate of 6% for the deposit and refurbishment monies, which would allow her to do the deal using none of her own money. She learnt how to approach her family in a professional manner and could provide sound evidence that she knew what she was doing in a clear and logical format.

Let's look at a clear breakdown of the numbers so you understand how they work in practice. Debbie borrowed the initial deposit monies of £17,587.50 (25% of the purchase price) as well as the fees and refurbishment money of £12,000 from a family member, paying them an interest rate of 6%. So in total, she borrowed £29,587.50 at 6% for a period of 12 months meaning she would pay £1,775.25 in interest to her investor as well as the mortgage payments of £2,625.75 over 12 months (£43,762.50 mortgage at 6% interest for 12 months). The monthly mortgage payment of £218.81 was something that she was happy to pay out of her own pocket as her salary allowed her to do this.

The reality of this is that by following a clear set of rules, she was able to finance a deal using none of her own money. By also getting a professional team on board to undertake the refurbishment, she was able to get the property finished within four weeks and ready for renting out. This provided her with an income immediately to cover the mortgage and give her cash flow whilst she waited six months in order to refinance the property. Therefore, she only had to pay the mortgage for a period of one month! This left her in a position where she owned a property which was in a high-demand area for rental and had strong equity in it. She then had the option of selling the deal on the open market and pocketing a lot of cash minus the costs of selling, or refinancing the deal at a later date and holding it for income.

If Debbie chose the refinancing option, she would be able to do so based on the market value of £105,000 of which she would be able to get a 75% loan to value mortgage of £78,750. Her original costs of doing the deal are £74,751 assuming she holds the property for the full year to refinance, which means she will cash out at around £3,999, less the fees for doing the refinance. Chances are, she will put between £1,000 and £2,000 in her pocket after this, so she will have been paid for buying a property! Not only that, if we look in detail at the cash flow on the property, the numbers look like this:

Monthly Rental Income	£650.00
Mortgage costs per month	£295.31
£105,000 x 75% =	£78,750
£78,750 x 4.5%	£3,543.75
£3,543.75 divided by 12 =	£295.31
Lettings Fee @ 15% of rent =	£97.50
Wear and Tear Allowance @ 10% of rent =	£65.00
Contingency @ 5% of rent =	£32.50
Total Investment Income	£159.69 per calendar month

The above figures are a wildly different story from those which we witnessed with Billy's deal earlier, which I hope demonstrates to you the value of education and what is possible when you know what you are doing. The question I have for you, as the reader, to consider is: *"If you can buy property with little or none of your own money, how many properties can you buy?"* You will probably come up with the answer: *"As many as I can find!"* which would be absolutely right! So I hope you are now feeling suitably inspired and motivated to start developing your own personal knowledge of how to invest in property and continue to use this so that you empower yourself to acquire great deals like Debbie's.

Interestingly, the last time I caught up with Debbie she was telling me that she is now in a position where she is structuring these sorts of deals for just £1 and getting her tenants to do the renovation work on the property for her! She is one smart lady and she is definitely showing others in this industry how it's done. One of the key reasons for her success, I believe, is that she is humble enough to admit that she doesn't know it all and continues to learn and improve her knowledge and understanding of property investing every single day. I would respectfully suggest that if it's the right approach for her, it might also be the right approach for you.

Now that we have covered how to buy right, you can see the importance of doing this correctly so that you can continually recycle your money in and out of each and every deal you buy. Nothing will slow your progress more or cause you to have an inefficient business as paying too much for each property. Here's a little secret: you get the same rent for the property whether you pay £100,000 for it or £50,000. However, the lower the purchase price, the lower your mortgage and associated outgoing costs, which in turn increases the amount of cash you put in your pocket every single month. Many people miss this important point and lock money into each property, which means they have to either earn or raise the next deposit and renovation monies for each further deal. The more money you need to raise, generally speaking the harder it is to do, so let's make life easy for ourselves and ensure we are buying right to begin with.

In terms of other ways to raise money, once you can demonstrate to people that you know what you are doing and can operate in a competent and effective manner, they are likely to trust you with their hard-earned cash! Always put yourself in the position of a lender of money and ask yourself the questions that you would ask if you were being approached for money. You need to remember that the one thing people have in their minds when you ask them for money is: are they ever going to see the money they lend you again? If the risk is perceived to be too high and the rewards you are offering too low, very few people are going to trust you with their money to invest in property.

Your closest friends and family members will be the ones to support you initially in your journey when it comes to buying property and potentially loaning you the money to start investing. Depending upon the mortgage lender you use, they may have to be a joint venture partner in the deal to pass the lender's criteria, so you will need to draw up a partnership agreement before going into the deal so you both know what is required upfront. A Joint Venture in this instance may well be that your friend or family member provides the money to do the deal and you find the property investment deal.

On this note, I will say that many partnerships and joint ventures fail in property, as well as other businesses, for the simple reason that people do not look far enough into the future when they are discussing the arrangement initially. They do not draw up a partnership agreement between the two parties which outlines their roles and responsibilities as well as the risks and rewards each party to the deal will face, depending upon the outcome. Unfortunately, many close friendships end because people verbally agree something which is not subsequently documented in writing, leading to reliance upon memories which fade with time, or misunderstandings in what will happen in certain circumstances. My word of advice here is to ensure everything is documented in writing so that you have something to fall back on at a later date should you ever need it. This will provide you with security and peace of mind.

To highlight this point, should I choose to get into business with a friend, we would both have to agree to and sign a carefully drafted partnership agreement, which runs to around 25 pages depending upon the business we are involved in. This truly does document everything from the sharing of profits or losses, roles and responsibilities for each business, as well as a lot of 'what if' scenarios that could possibly happen in the future which would affect either or both parties' ability to operate effectively in the business. There is also a mechanism for exiting the business should either party decide to do so. If you would like more information on setting up a partnership agreement, I will happily provide you with a free copy of my guide if you visit the following wesbite: www.assafeashouses.com

You should always approach your friends and family in a professional manner and remember that there will potentially be a lot of money at stake, so always act as professionally as possible so you win their confidence. Ideally, you should approach them with some form of investment summary document which outlines an example of what you are seeking to do and the involvement you are seeking from your investing partners. One thing that you need to be fully aware of is that the FCA heavily regulate the borrowing and advertisement for borrowing of money in the UK, so you need to be absolutely crystal clear in your approach to ensure you do not fall foul of their regulation which could lead to a heavy fine or potential imprisonment if you break the law! Clearly this is something that we all wish to avoid, so make sure you read up on the rules and regulations so that you keep yourself safe. As I always say, it's a lot easier to make money out of prison than in!

After friends and family come Angel investors, who are people who have money and are considered high net worth individuals as far as the FCA are concerned. You will probably know of a few of these people, although they may not necessarily be part of your social or professional circles at this stage. Do not let this stop you! Angels are always short of good investment opportunities that will provide a great reward for them, so they are well worth approaching in a professional manner to see if they would consider investing on a joint venture basis with you. Be warned, however, approaching these types of people to borrow money will not be an easy thing, and they will certainly put you through your paces and ask lots of questions that you had better know the answers to if you are expecting them to invest with you. Whilst this might frighten some people away from having a discussion with them, I know that you will want to take on this challenge because it will be an opportunity to learn, grow and do better next time if you are not successful in winning them over the first time around.

There are numerous other ways to raise finance for investing which are beyond the scope of this book; however I will say that raising money for the right deal is easy. If you are struggling to raise the money for a deal, then I would suggest that you might not have a deal.

CHAPTER SIX

Surveying The Property

As a surveyor myself, I felt that it was apt to add a chapter to the book regarding surveys and valuations on properties and what is involved, as in my experience this is the one area that many investors know very little about and it appears to be shrouded in mystery by the surveying profession! I hear many different views on the benefits or otherwise of having surveys and valuations performed on properties, and a lot of people do not see the value of having an independent, impartial and professional pair of eyes view the property as they feel they know what they are looking for.

Unfortunately, in my experience, this isn't the case. To my mind, I will tell you that an independent survey and valuation is as important as using a solicitor to buy the property. There are so many instances I have encountered over my time as a property investor where people have lost a huge sum of money by thinking they knew what they are doing, however they have bought properties that needed significant structural work which was unseen at the time of viewing the property. Some rookie investors have bought properties which were unmortgageable, and as a result ended up leaving all their money in the property as they decided to buy it for cash. In the worst instances, I have known rookies buy properties on a bridging loan, which ended up costing them a small fortune on a monthly basis because they couldn't refinance away from the bridging loan onto a traditional mortgage due to the lack of structural integrity within the property.

All told, not knowing the structural condition of the property you are considering buying can be the single biggest mistake you can make. The problem with getting a survey done after you have bought the property for cash is that there is no course for redress on the seller as the usual *caveat emptor* (buyer beware) applies. It is assumed that you know what you are doing and you have had every opportunity to inspect or have the property surveyed before you purchase it.

The main benefit of getting a professional survey on a property is that it provides you with enormous peace of mind that everything which is or might be wrong with the property is fully documented in a comprehensive report that you can review and pass onto your builder to ensure you have accounted for all items of work required. If you have missed something which will affect your potential profit margins, etc., you are in a strong position because you can then renegotiate with the seller in light of the findings in the surveyors report, or pull out of the purchase of the property if the findings are significant. The main advantage of using the report as a negotiating point is that the seller knows, if you don't buy the property, anyone else coming along to buy it will find the same problems with the property based on another surveyor looking at the property.

When you have a comprehensive report on what is wrong with the property, you can discuss this with your builder or refurbishment team so you can be sure that you are addressing all the defects and not missing anything which might later cost you thousands of pounds to rectify once you are on site doing the refurbishment works. I know lots of experienced investors who have missed typical things such as rising damp in the internal walls, which only came to light when the builder was on site refurbishing the property. The problem with missing something like this and not planning for it is that it not only affects your budget but also the order and timescale of the proposed renovation works. Rising damp remedial works require several weeks of drying out time before the walls can be re-plastered, which would seriously impact the timescale of completing things like decoration and finding a tenant.

What survey options are there?

This is a question I am asked frequently, so in order to give you the most comprehensive answer, I will tell you about them all and describe some pros and cons of each one in turn. Your options as a property investor are to go for a straightforward Valuation of the property; a Homebuyers Report; a Building Survey; or a Structural Survey.

Valuation – As the name suggests, this is a basic inspection of the property to confirm that it actually exists and what it is worth on the open market. When you take out a mortgage on the property you are buying, the lender will require a valuation to be carried out which is something you will pay for. Please note, however, this is an inspection to cover the lender's interests and not yours! The valuation surveyor does not inspect any of the structural elements of the property, which most people do not know! Clearly, if there are obvious structural defects on the property, the surveyor will request another report from a Building or Structural Surveyor to clarify these issues before they give you a valuation on the property. Does this cause you any problems? Well, the short answer is yes, it can do. The main issues you will be faced with are potentially paying twice for two surveyors to look at the property, together with associated delays in getting two people to look around the property and submit their reports. This may pose you a particular problem if you require your mortgage to go through within a tight timeframe. I would always caution people against getting just a valuation done on a property that they are arranging bridging finance against. If the valuation surveyor doesn't comment on something that later stops you from getting a mortgage on the property, to pay back the bridging loan, you will be well and truly stuck and paying thousands of pounds in finance costs to try and get out of this situation!

Homebuyers Report – This is a more in-depth inspection of the property, and I would recommend that you should be looking to get this type of inspection and report done on every property you buy as an absolute minimum. Ideally you should get a Homebuyers Report on any property up to 80 years of age unless it is a complete wreck and requires substantial renovation (in which case

I would get a Building Survey done). What I really like about the Homebuyers Report is that it is produced from a standard RICS template and as such is very easy for absolute beginners to read and understand. There are also plenty of illustrations to explain any technical language used by the surveyors throughout their report. Therefore it is very clear to read, understand and interpret and is well respected in the property industry.

Building Survey – This is the most in-depth inspection of any property and such reports are the most expensive on the market due to the time required to inspect the property and assemble the report. I would seriously recommend these to any nervous or cautious investor, or anyone buying a property which requires a lot of renovation or is in excess of 80 years old. The report will be very comprehensive and therefore will cover all elements of concern that the surveyor has about the property which will stand you in good stead when you are planning your renovation and refurbishment works.

Structural Survey – The structural survey is usually reserved for properties which show signs of structural movement (such as cracking to brickwork, or sloping floor), and will usually be recommended as a further inspection and report by any surveyor doing a valuation or Homebuyers Report on a property in order to clear up any specific concerns they may have about the property. It would also be used if there is any damage on your property resulting from subsidence or movement and will be required as part of a negotiation with your buildings insurance company.

The above summary of each report should give you clear

guidance on which will be suitable for your requirements for the properties you are buying. One word of caution, however: always assume the worst when you are buying a property and cover yourself by getting in the professionals to look at the property before you buy it. This is particularly important if you are buying a property which is going to auction. If the report doesn't find anything wrong with the property and gives it a clean bill of health, then believe me when I say this is money well spent! The worst thing that could happen is thinking that there is nothing wrong with the property, not getting a survey carried out on it, and then finding later that there is a problem that will stop you from either selling it or getting a mortgage on it (or in the worst cases, both!).

I worked with clients who were thinking about buying a property via the modern method of auction (something I would encourage everyone *not* to do!), and because they were in a rush to buy the property, they were going to get the survey done *after* they had exchanged contracts on it. Thankfully I was able to intervene and told them not to buy it until we got a surveyor around the property to check it out. They were glad we did! The surveyor found significant structural issues with the property, which resulted in him classing the property as unmortgageable! This was great news for my clients as we were able to protect their investment of over £140,000 by not buying a property which could not be sold on or refinanced at a later date. I can tell you they were very grateful to have my input on this one!

There are a couple of other things that I want you to be aware of when it comes to being an expert investor in property and they involve the issue of valuations on the property you are thinking of buying. As the credit-crunch-fuelled recession has continued, surveyors and lenders have become more and more cautious and, as such, surveyors are putting conservative valuations on properties, rather than ambitious or even fair valuation figures, and this is causing some issues for investors as properties are being 'down-valued' at the point of re-mortgage or refinance. This is something that I have experienced personally and you need to know about to make sure you are protected in what you are doing.

A few years ago, I was literally the only person buying investment properties in my area. This was fine as I was picking up properties at big discounts. However, when the valuation surveyor came to look at a property for re-mortgage, the only comparables they could use for the valuation report were other properties that I had bought at a deep discount! This caused me a real problem as I had effectively created a lower market value by buying properties as such rock-bottom prices that the surveyors could not justify higher valuations as no-one else was buying property! Therefore I had to sit back for a while and let rookie investors pay a higher market value for some properties in order to restore the market to its former price before I could refinance.

The second thing I want you to be aware of is what is known as the '90-day sale valuation', which is something that the valuation surveyor comments on when he initially inspects the property for mortgage or refinance purposes. What this is in practice is the surveyor's opinion of how much the property will sell for based on having a 90-day period to achieve a sale. Clearly, if you have a tight time limit on selling a property, the likelihood is that the property will have to be sold at a discount to achieve a sale within the 90-day period. Typically, this discount would be between 10% and 20% depending upon the area where the property is located. However, most lenders are now choosing to lend against the 90-day sale value rather than the market value, which can result in investors being caught out by receiving less money from their mortgage company than they had initially hoped for. The consequence of this is that it is likely to lock some, if not all, of your deposit into the property, which could seriously hamper your progress as a property investor. It's something to be aware of and is unlikely to go away until the property market improves significantly.

What am I looking for when viewing a property?

As a surveyor, I am regularly asked this question, so I thought it would be an opportune moment to share some important pointers with you on what to look for when viewing the property, as this will help you to avoid some common pitfalls and also draw your attention to areas that you may not have been aware of previously which need further inspection from a professional surveyor. It is not my intention to turn you into a surveyor with the information provided here, nor am I suggesting that by including this information that you do not need to have a surveyor inspect the property. This would be folly; I am a surveyor and I do not survey any properties myself that I am thinking of buying! This is because of the potential for emotional attachment to the property which I choose to overcome by getting someone independent and impartial to survey it, rather than running the risk of costing myself several thousands of pounds by missing something that I didn't want to see because I wanted the deal more!

When I first arrive at the property, I always do a quick inspection of the outside from the front, in order to build a picture of how well the property has been cared for. Some unscrupulous people will cover up internal cracks or issues within a property, but very few of the same people will think to mask potential issues externally. I typically stand back from the property, and if it is a terraced or semi-detached house, this will usually involve viewing the property from the other side of the road (remember your Green Cross Code here!). If you have a pair of binoculars, this is to your advantage. I then do a top-down inspection of the front elevation which starts at the top of the roof and works its way down to the ground level.

What I am looking for are things like the following:

- Is the ridge line of the roof straight and true?

- Does the roof bow or dish in any parts?

- Are the gutters full of debris or overflowing?

- Is the chimneystack (if present) in good condition or does it have plants/trees growing out of it?

- Are there any missing pieces of the roof covering?

- Are the flashings (leadwork adjacent to changes in roof height or penetrations such as a chimneystack) to the roof in good order?

- What condition are the windows and door(s) in?

- Does the front wall of the property exhibit any

cracking to the brickwork or render coat (if present)?

- Does the property have evidence of a damp proof course at low level? Or evidence of one installed in recent months/years?

- Is there anything within close proximity to the property which would cause me some concern or warrant further investigation such as overhead power lines, electricity substations, sewage works, water in the form of rivers or ponds/lakes which might present a flooding risk, noisy or offensive neighbours, junk piled up nearby either in neighbouring properties or streets, the general feel and safety of the local area, any obvious defects on neighbouring properties such as cracking to brickwork or boarded up windows?

Once I have cast a critical eye over the front of the property, I will do the same inspection and pose the same questions at the rear and potentially side(s) of the property if external access permits. Clearly, in terraced homes this would be difficult, but the front and rear elevations will reveal most things that are potentially wrong with these types of properties. Once I have viewed the external elements and taken lots of photographs as a reminder, I will then move onto a comprehensive internal inspection backed up again with photographs. On this point, it is worthwhile obtaining permission from the owner or agent selling the property that they are happy with you taking photographs, as some people are very uncomfortable with this, so make sure you don't get onto the wrong foot with them as this will undoubtedly hamper your negotiations at a later date!

With regard to the internal inspection of the property, I will look at the overall condition of the decoration as well as the kitchen and bathroom fitments to determine if they will need to be replaced before the property can be rented out. My personal take on this is that properties with new kitchens and bathrooms tend to rent more quickly and the tenants tend to stay longer, compared to those where investors have tried to cut corners and do things on the cheap. When I am walking around the property I will also do the following to understand the structure and condition at a deeper level:

- **Floors** – On the ground floor of the property, stamp or jump on the floor in areas like the sitting room and hallway (not the kitchen if it has a tiled floor!), to see if the property has a suspended timber floor or a concrete floor. It will be easy to tell the difference as one will move under your body weight and the other won't! What we are looking for here is excessive movement of the timber floor which may indicate floor joists that are close to failing through rot or decay and will need to be replaced in the future. This can be a very expensive job and cause you some issues if not found early on in the course of the proposed purchase. If the floor is solid, is it level or is it uneven when you walk across it? If it is showing signs of being uneven, this will need further inspection, as it may need to be replaced.

- **Walls** – When you are walking around the property, look at the plaster finish on the walls. Is it in good condition or is it full of holes or cracks? Cracks could potentially be a sign of something more serious and will need further investigation. Does the property have an Artex finish to the wall so it looks like the decoration on a Christmas cake? This can make the property difficult to rent and will ideally need to be re-plastered to a smooth and even finish; the cost of this will need to be factored into your budget. I would also be quite suspicious of any property which is in the process of being 'renovated for sale'. This may involve the seller trying to cover up some problems through re-plastering or filling cracks and redecorating internally. Always get a professional to look at the property if you suspect this is the case. One giveaway can be to look into all built-in cupboards and wardrobes, as most people who are trying to conceal something miss these areas and any cracking will be obvious when you open the door. You should also tap the walls and listen for any hollow sounds which may indicate that the plasterwork is losing adhesion to the brickwork and, as such, may need to be replaced.

- **Doors** – Always look at the internal doors and doorframes and see how well the door matches up to the doorframe when it is closed. This can be a dead giveaway if the property has moved, as either the door doesn't close properly in the doorframe, or the door has been modified in some way to make it fit which will be easy to spot as it will not be square and true. If you have any concerns here, keep a keen eye on the rest of the property when you are walking around, as there may be other signs of movement within the property.

- **Ceilings** – As with the walls, look at the condition of the ceilings to see if they have any cracking present, which may need further investigation, or an Artex finish which needs to be covered. Any gaps between the ceiling and the wall will also be a sure sign that something is not quite right, so look out for this.

- **Electrical installation** – Whilst I appreciate you are probably not a qualified domestic electrician, I will advise you to pay attention to the condition of the light and electrical sockets as well as the main fuse board within the property. If the wiring to lights looks dated (the biggest give-away is rubber cabling or two thin wires that are twisted together) or the fuse board is the old-fashioned type with re-wirable fuses, the property will undoubtedly need its wiring brought up to date in line with modern regulations. This can be quite an expensive job, so be sure to budget for this in your works. Also be aware that modern living requires quite a lot of energy within each room, so you must ensure that there are at least two to three double sockets per room, otherwise your tenants will be running everything off extension leads which could be a potential fire hazard.

- **Heating Installation** – Take a good look at the condition of the boiler and radiators within the property (assuming that it already has central heating – if it does not, you will have to allow for this in your refurbishment programme and budget) and assess the visual condition of the fitments. If the heating system still has a separate hot water cylinder as well as radiators that are showing signs of rust, it is likely that the boiler and radiators will need to be replaced with a more energy-efficient installation. Tenants are becoming increasingly aware of the costs of heating and running a property, so they are looking for properties that have high energy efficient installations, and if your property doesn't have these, you may struggle to rent it out.

- **Kitchen and bathroom** – As I am sure you are aware, the kitchen and bathroom in a property are generally what sell it, so it is important to ensure these areas of the house are in good condition. It doesn't cost huge money to supply and fit a contract white bathroom suite or a trade kitchen which can be bought from a good supplier at reasonable cost. This not only adds significantly to the appeal of the property, making it easier to sell or rent in the future, it is likely that you will give the tenant the message that you care about the condition of the property which in turn means they will look after it for you and stay longer as a result.

If you pay attention when you look around the property on your first viewing, you will get a good feel as to whether or not the property has been looked after and which areas require further investigation. This should help you work on some budget figures for the renovation works so you can begin negotiating the purchase of the property, and then bring a surveyor in at a later date once the price has been agreed so you can be sure that you haven't missed anything. One thing I will say is to be careful who is guiding you on the renovation works required to the property. Quite simply, if a surveyor neglects to mention something on a property that costs you money, he has professional indemnity insurance in place which you can potentially make a claim against depending on the severity of the omission. But if your builder is advising you and misses something or doesn't mention something which later costs you thousands of pounds to rectify, you have very little course for redress from him.

Now that we know what to look for when viewing a property, let's take a look at what's involved in the actual purchase of a property so you can understand how all the pieces of the jigsaw fit together to give you the overall big picture.

CHAPTER SEVEN

The Buying Process

Hopefully by now you have been a busy investor and done lots of research and looked at lots of properties and made plenty of offers. Then the worst thing imaginable happens – someone turns around and says 'yes' to your offer! This is the area where I see most new investors panic, and it's not until you have bought your first half-a-dozen or so properties that this feeling goes away. What is it about this situation that makes so many investors nervous? I think it's the one area where suddenly everything becomes very real and you have to perform based on your word and the commitments you have made to the seller of the property. There will also be enormous self-doubt on the first few deals where you will question yourself if you have paid too much for the property or if you have budgeted enough to cover the remedial works required to bring the property up to standard. You may also question whether or not you can raise a mortgage or whether you will be able to find a tenant or buyer when the project is completed! These are perfectly normal concerns that almost everyone experiences. Assuming you follow the guidance within the pages of this book, you will be well prepared to deal with all of these questions.

For the purposes of this chapter, I am going to assume that you are buying the property from a private seller who is selling their property via an estate agent. The same process is broadly applicable if you are buying the property through other methods, so you will be safe if you follow the guidance given here. Once you have inspected the property, you will make an offer based on where the property works for you financially taking into account the level of works required to bring it up to standard. If your offer is accepted via the estate agent, you will be required to provide the agent with details of the solicitor who will be acting on your behalf in the purchase of the property. (Please take note of my advice here: even if you are a solicitor who has the skills to do the purchase of the property yourself, I would encourage you not to do so, as you should be concentrating on finding the deals and finding the money to buy the properties. In any event, any lender is unlikely to let you do this if you are getting a mortgage on the property.)

As with any stage of the property buying process, it is important to use professionals who will follow your instructions or will find ways to make things happen that you want to have happen in relation to the property purchase. The wrong solicitor on board will make your business hard work and not give you the results that you require. For instance, Jayne was a rookie investor who explained to me that her solicitor told her that doing things like a 'keys undertaking' or a 'delayed completion' were 'illegal', and wouldn't act for her unless she did exactly what he wanted to do on the proposed purchase of the property. Such limited, and frankly incorrect, thinking on the part of a solicitor will hinder your progress tremendously; unfortunately, most people will not challenge what a solicitor says, as they are deemed to be 'professionals' whose opinion you do not question! Nothing could be further from the truth – when these people are acting for you they should be guiding you using their experience and legal knowledge, rather than stopping you from doing something by saying it's 'illegal' or 'you can't do that' because they lack the knowledge and experience to make it happen, or the forethought to take on an idea and look at how to make it work within the scope of the law, rather than just saying no!

Once you have provided the agents with your solicitor's details, they will more than likely issue the 'Memorandum of Sale' document, which is issued to yourself and the seller as well as the solicitors who are acting on behalf of you both. This will provide them with basic details of the property as well as the purchase price and any special terms that are applicable to the deal. Your solicitor will then liaise with you regarding the steps involved in the purchase and will more than likely require some money to be put on account so they can begin their work on your behalf. At this stage, I would talk openly and frankly with your solicitor about the proposed timescales for the transaction and any particular time constraints that may be involved. The earlier they know about this, the easier it will be for them to help you in the transaction.

It is also at this stage that you want to explain to the solicitor that you would like to negotiate a 'keys undertaking' with the seller if you haven't been able to negotiate it via the estate agent. This is a period of time between the legal exchange of contracts and the practical completion of the purchase where you are able to access the property to undertake works. Depending on the condition of the property, these may be essential works to enable you to obtain a mortgage on it, or you may even be able to get consent to do the full renovation and refurbishment to the property before you have to pay for it! The benefit of this is that you can start marketing the property for sale or rent before you start paying the mortgage on it! A word of caution, however; I would never undertake works to a property which you haven't got a legal agreement in place for, as you are completely exposed and at risk financially should anything go wrong and the legal exchange of contracts does not actually take place.

Your solicitor should be taking on board your instructions in this regard and negotiating the undertaking with the seller's solicitors so that you have this in place before you exchange contracts. This may save you a few months of time, allowing you to complete the renovation works before you get the mortgage, or even to find a buyer or tenant before you take ownership of the property. However, do not put a tenant into a property that you do not own, or sign an agreement to the same until you have completed the purchase of the property! (When you become skilled at doing this, you can drastically cut down your void periods on properties you buy. I have had a void period of two hours between completing on the property at 1pm in the afternoon and a tenant moving in at 3pm after a new carpet had been fitted!)

Your solicitor will be responsible for checking over and reviewing the legal contract for the purchase of the property, which will be prepared by the seller's solicitor. Most properties are inevitably sold via standard contracts, which solicitors are used to reading time and again. When the seller's solicitor is saying they are 'drawing up the contract', this is not a time-intensive operation and can literally be done in less than an hour using the template and a word processor! Your solicitor will make sure that your interests are protected by reviewing the contract on your behalf and simultaneously applying for 'the searches' for the property.

The searches are enquiries made to local utility companies, the Local Authority and The Coal Authority about things that either have happened previously, or are planned to happen, or will be happening soon, which could affect the property you are buying in some way. These organisations have to notify your solicitor of anything likely to have an impact on the property, and therefore your solicitor will discuss these with you if they feel anything is going to hinder your future ownership of the property or your future plans. For example, if you are buying a property on the edge of town which enjoys a nice outlook over fields, you need to know if the Local Authority is planning on building a bypass or other major road over this land, or if a large developer has put in for planning permission to build on this land. This information should all be brought up on the searches.

Factors that may impact on your purchase or affect the value of your investment are things like the proximity of an electrical substation near to the property (some valuation surveyors are suggesting this could devalue a property by as much as 25% in the current market, depending on the proximity of the station to the property in question), as well as the proximity of any mineshafts from previous coal mining in the area which could affect your ability to obtain a mortgage on the property.

One of the other duties of care that the solicitor has is to act on behalf of the mortgage lender in the security of their funds against the legal title of the property. Your solicitor will be involved in transferring the title (ownership) of the property from the seller's name into your name with the assistance of the Land Registry. At the same time, he will be required to secure the loan or mortgage against the legal title of the property, which will basically prevent you from selling the property without the lender being paid back their money! The property effectively becomes their security, which they will repossess if you fail to keep up the repayments on the mortgage or other loan secured on it.

One of my biggest tips to give you ultimate flexibility in your purchasing of properties, is to suggest that you arrange for the contracts to be drafted in your name "and/or assigns". What this effectively means is that you are creating a legal contract, which is assignable to a third party at your discretion. Therefore you are in a position to be able to find another buyer to buy the property should you wish to. The beautiful part about this is that it gives you flexibility – if you cannot buy it for whatever reason (i.e. you can't get a mortgage or your deposit funds are tied up in other deals), you are able to source the deal onto another buyer and claim a fee for doing so. This protects your interests and helps you to keep your word with the seller or agent involved in selling the property as long as the buyer you are working with is reliable and willing to keep to your original promises.

Of course, you may just decide to source property deals onto other people and take a fee for it, and this can work very well for you if you do things in the right manner. I know of many people who do this well and they make at least £1,500 per property deal, with some making £7,000 to £10,000 per deal as they are providing a full suite of services including finding the deal, managing it through to completion, project managing the refurbishment and then finding a tenant for the property at the end of it all. The good news for you is that most other people who are looking to buy property whom you will meet at networking events, etc., will not have the same strategy as you have because you have read this book and are approaching investing from a very savvy mindset. Other investors that you meet will be prepared to leave money in deals or will not want as much discount as you (they may be happy with 10%-15% discounts), so even if a deal doesn't work for you, it can work beautifully for other people. Now, this is not an excuse to rip off other people by selling them a bad deal, as you will only be as good as your reputation (which could be tarnished from this point on), however it does put you in a strong position to be able to create money either from buying the deal in the first place or sourcing it on for a fee.

One of the primary reasons for using a solicitor to protect your interests is because Land Registry fraud is becoming increasingly common with every year that passes and unscrupulous individuals have been known to sell properties that do not actually belong to them! It would cause you a massive problem if you were the one that agreed to buy a property, you got the mortgage on it and then later found out that you did not own the property because the person who sold it to you didn't actually own it in the first place! Please make sure your solicitor does a thorough job in researching the title and ensuring that whoever is selling the property to you actually owns it!

Once your solicitor has done the legal legwork to check the property is what it is supposed to be and you have your finance in place, they will be prepared to let you sign the contract in preparation for legal exchange of contracts. Now, many solicitors will tell you that the minimum amount of money that you can use to exchange contracts, in order to make the whole deal legally binding, is 10% of the purchase price of the property. In fact, the legal minimum that is required by British law is actually just £1! So, in order to keep tight reins on the whole property purchase, I am going to encourage you to exchange contracts with as little deposit as possible, and go for as long a gap as you can between the exchange of contracts and the practical completion of the purchase of the property when the balance of the purchase price becomes payable to the seller.

Be warned that once you have exchanged contracts on the property, you are legally bound to purchase it, so you cannot withdraw from the purchase. Therefore you need to be absolutely certain that you have everything lined up, as failing to complete on the purchase will have some very severe consequences. In addition, if you are thinking about buying properties from auction, I can tell you that the moment the auctioneer's hammer falls and hits the desk or pedestal, you are legally bound to buy the property as you have exchanged contracts at the moment your bid is accepted. So you need to make sure all your due diligence has been completed before you go to the auction to bid, because if anything is incorrect about the property in the future, you will be unable to purchase it but still be bound by the legal contract which will result in the seller suing you for a substantial amount of damages.

Taking a step back for a moment, once your offer has been accepted and solicitors have been instructed, this is the time when you will be speaking with your mortgage broker or other finance house in order to set the wheels in motion to get the finance together to buy the property. You will usually get a 'Decision in Principle' from the lender you are thinking about getting a mortgage from, which basically means, subject to valuation and credit checks, they will grant you a mortgage to buy the property. This will be the point at which you will pay for a valuation on the property. However, I would not suggest that you should be paying mortgage brokers' fees at this stage until the mortgage has been drawn down.

It is important to mention a few points here for the sake of clarity and to avoid confusion for those of you who are not familiar with buying property in the current marketplace. Mortgage companies will not lend you 100% of the purchase price of the property for a buy-to-let property; they will usually limit their contribution to between 50% and 75% of the value of the property, or the purchase price, whichever is the lower figure. This causes some new investors confusion, because they feel that as they are buying the property for £60,000 but it is worth £100,000, they will get a mortgage based on the property value of £100,000, not the £60,000 purchase price. In an ideal world, that would be a lovely thing; however, I am the bearer of bad news when I tell you that they will make their decision to lend based on purchase price or valuation, whichever is the lower of the two!

The reason why lenders will not lend the full 100% of the purchase price of the property is because they want you to have some 'money on the line'. You probably won't find that terminology mentioned in any of their advertising or marketing literature, but they do not want to be taking all the risk of the property ownership. If they have all their money in the property and you have none, if the market takes a nosedive in the future, you could walk away and leave the bank or mortgage company to sort out the problem and you would have suffered very little financial loss.

This is another reason why it is so important to negotiate a good discount on the property in order to put you in a stronger position to refinance the property in the future and to pull most, if not all, of your deposit and refurbishment money out of the deal. Another benefit is that you also protect yourself in the future, as any falls in market value will only affect your equity in the property rather than your cash deposit, and the risk of entering negative equity is greatly reduced.

Something I will say is, be careful who you trust as your mortgage broker, as inevitably, when you go and speak with most estate agents, they will try and railroad you into speaking with their mortgage advisor/broker. Not all of these brokers are able to access all of the mortgages available on the open market, and therefore they may recommend products to you that are more financially beneficial to them (in the form of the commissions they make), than to you as the client! This doesn't happen with all brokers, but it's something to be aware of. In my experience, most mortgage brokers working for an estate agency will not understand how you work as a professional property investor, and therefore will not be able to provide you with the guidance you need in order to build your portfolio in the fastest and best manner possible. My advice is: secure a mortgage broker via recommendation who understands how property investors work, so he can talk openly about your strategy first of all, before recommending the appropriate finance products which match your needs and requirements rather than what is in his own financial interest.

Once the mortgage company has been chosen and has issued the preliminary Decision in Principle for you, you will usually be required to pay for the valuation to take place on the property to check that it is worth what you are going to be paying for it. Remember that this is to protect the lender's interests rather than yours! However, once the valuation has been carried out and the surveyor is happy that the property is worth what you are paying for it, the surveyor will confirm this to the mortgage company who will then issue you a mortgage offer – after they have conducted any final checks which may include a credit check on you to ensure that you are credit worthy, can handle your finances and meet the mortgage payments every month.

The mortgage offer will usually be sent to both your mortgage broker as well as your solicitor, and once your solicitor is in receipt of this document, has conducted the remainder of the searches, has completed any pre-contract enquiries and is in receipt of your deposit, you will be in a position to exchange contracts. Now, when you are speaking with estate agents and solicitors, they will tell you many times that they are "trying to exchange contracts on the deal, however there are delays in doing so". The actual exchange of contracts is nothing more than a phone call process between the two solicitors, who acknowledge the legal exchange of contracts by noting the date and time of the phone call on the front of the legal contract! It is literally nothing more complicated than this, therefore there is nothing to stop you getting contracts exchanged quite quickly on a property deal as long as all the paperwork is in order.

You may decide to exchange contracts and complete the purchase of the property (when the balance of the funds gets paid to the seller) at the same time, or within a short time period of a few days to a few weeks, or you may decide to introduce a longer time delay between exchange and completion. This is perfectly legal, as long as it has been agreed as part of the legal negotiations and forms part of the contract documentation that has been exchanged. At this point, you will get the keys and be able to gain access to the property in order to start your renovation works and exercise your investment strategy on the property. It is also the point when the mortgage funds will be drawn down just prior to completion by your solicitor and paid across to the seller, so you will start incurring interest.

Now that we have a clear idea on how the solicitors are involved in the purchase and sale of a property, let's take a look at how we renovate a property for maximum profit.

CHAPTER EIGHT

The Renovation and Refurbishment Process

By now, you should have a clear understanding of the stages involved in the purchase of properties and know how to find the deals and how to buy them at a price that works for you and your business. The part of the process that we are going to cover now is the one area where most new investors can really sink themselves, and it's certainly the one area where rookie investors cost themselves a fortune.

Despite the fact that Sarah Beeney and programmes such as *Homes Under The Hammer* and *DIY SOS* have made renovating a property look easy, the reality is that on your first few projects you are going to be faced with quite a few challenges which need to be met head-on in order for your proposed renovation project to succeed. Some of you may be thinking that you will short-cut the process by buying properties that are already done up, but the problem with this is that you are not adding value to the property during your ownership, so you will find it quite difficult to get an increased valuation on the property in six months' time when you come to refinance it to recover your costs and your deposit. Ideally, the properties you are buying to build your portfolio will need to have some element of renovation in order to increase their value. You will also find it easier to buy properties at a discounted price that need work doing to them, as it is easier to justify the lower offer due to the work needed.

One of the key issues that new investors face when renovating a property is the desire to renovate the property to their own tastes rather than what is required for the marketplace. The danger here is the emotional attachment, which causes them to overspend on the property by putting a jacuzzi in the bathroom and installing a Christie's kitchen with built-in appliances and granite worktops in their two-bedroom terraced house in Hull!! This may sound extreme, but I have seen many examples where new investors have been swayed by their emotions to buy and install expensive kitchens and bathrooms which all adds to the costs and will ultimately affect your bottom line. Furthermore, your individual tastes may well be against what the market actually wants, and you will find it harder to rent your property or sell it for the price you want if you haven't paid attention to market norms.

Remember that you are operating at a level which is 'fit for purpose' with your property renovations, and you are not doing it to live in yourself. However, that does not mean that you do a substandard job on the renovations, or you offer poor-quality accommodation. What you are aiming to achieve is a standard of accommodation that you would be happy to live in yourself. If you listen to your intuition, you will not offer squalor, nor will you renovate your properties to be like Buckingham Palace! It will be to a standard, which will look clean, tidy and presentable and will be a blank canvas which your tenants or buyers can create a home from, rather than have your stamp of individualism.

Another key mistake that investors make is the order of works to renovate a property, as most new investors lack the experience of being able to refurbish a property to a good standard in a short space of time. In order to keep you safe in this process, let's take a look at the order in which the property should be renovated:

- **Strip out and 'demolition'** – Timescale 1-3 days – I have put the word demolition in inverted commas as I do not want you to take on too much work on your first couple of projects, as they can be money-pits that drain you of cash if you do not know what you are doing or you do not have reliable trades people you can count on who will quote the job accurately for you. That said, there might be elements of the property that need to be attended to, such as the removal or repositioning of an internal wall to improve the layout of the accommodation. If you are planning to do this type of work, ensure that you have consulted an appropriate professional (structural engineer) who can advise you if the wall is structurally load-bearing or not. The last thing you want to do is remove a wall and the rest of the house falls down (this has happened, particularly when people do not understand the nature of structural load-bearing walls). The strip-out element will include such things as removing the existing kitchen and bathroom (assuming these are to be replaced), as well as any old carpets, wall-coverings and flooring you are not planning to retain. It is during this stage that certain items of work may arise which were not immediately clear during the initial inspection of the property, so I would always budget 15% more for your renovation costs by way of a contingency in order to keep yourself safe. If something does crop up that you were not expecting, talk with your builder and trades people regarding the issue and the proposed solution to put it right. Make sure you are using a Gas Safe engineer if your gas boiler is to be replaced and you are stripping out any gas appliances from the property. The last thing you want is to put anyone at risk by trying to cut corners. It goes without saying that this is one stage in the refurbishment where the danger of injury to people can be quite high, so make sure that you and your trades people are exercising appropriate caution to avoid accident or injury. I would also caution you against doing any of the renovation works yourself on your properties, especially if you are competent at DIY or you are a trades person yourself. Your skills as a property investor are finding deals and finding money, so trying to save a few pounds during the renovation will mean you are likely missing out on deals which will cost you several thousands of pounds in the long run.

- **Damp-proof works** – Timescale 1 to 4 weeks (including drying out time) – Hand in hand with the strip-out from the property is making a start on any damp-proof works that need to be carried out. If your property needs to have work undertaken on the ground floor in order to cure a rising damp problem, this will more than likely involve the removal of the plaster covering to the internal face of the walls up to a height of around a metre. Not only is this a messy job in its own right, you will also have to think about the treatment process, which could involve injection treatment of the walls with a damp-proofing solution, two render coats, a waterproofing layer and plaster finish. Depending on the time of year, this could take several weeks to dry out and therefore, if not started as one of the first jobs on the project, could affect the timescale of completing the property and getting it let. So, employ a suitable timber and damp-proofing professional to undertake all aspects of the work so they can provide a guarantee for the work once it is complete.

- **Replacement external doors and windows** – Timescale 1 to 2 days – Should the property you acquire have timber windows or old aluminium double-glazed windows, you would be well placed to replace these with new uPVC double-glazed windows which will not only be very energy efficient, but will also look good and make it easier for you to rent or sell your property. Shop around for your best deal on these as the costs can vary greatly depending upon your supplier. They need to be changed early on in your project, as the removal of the old windows could damage surrounding plasterwork. Be careful to check if the new uPVC windows need to have steel lintels placed above them in order to support the brickwork, otherwise the brickwork will eventually sag onto the top of the window, causing cracking to the brickwork and making it impossible to open or close the window at a later date. You will also need to ensure that the contractor who installs the windows is able to provide you with a FENSA certificate to comply with building regulations.

- **Rewiring and re-plumbing** – Timescale 7 to 14 days – If you are planning on doing a rewire and a re-plumb to your house, then I would suggest that your trades people start this work early on in the process once the strip out has been completed. This will almost always involve the first-floor floorboards being taken up, so that the plumber and electricians can get to the floor joists to drill them and run the wires and pipe work throughout the property where they won't be seen. Be aware that, depending on the time of year of your project, you may be in a position where your plumber in particular is very busy, so make sure you book all tradesmen in advance. This is something that you can programme in whilst your solicitor is buying the property for you. If you are planning to do a full rewire, this can be a particularly messy job, as the plaster on the walls will be channelled in order to bury the wires in the wall for practicality as well as aesthetics. One tip on the plumbing side of things is that I would encourage you to opt for plastic pipework rather than copper. There are two very good reasons for this: the first is that plastic is easier to work with and will speed up the installation for you and reduce costs. The second is that copper is valuable and, if your property is empty, at any point you may notice that some unscrupulous individuals will break in and strip the copper out in order to sell it! This is never done with any kind of care and, whilst they are only stealing copper worth a small amount, the damage to your property from running water for several hours overnight will be substantial.

Always use a Gas Safe plumber to install the boiler for you and ensure that you are issued with an installation certificate so that you are covered. You will also be required to do an annual gas safety check at the property if you decide to keep it and rent it out. This is a legal requirement and, without it, you could be prosecuted. Any new electrical work that you have done should also come with an NICEIC compliant installation certificate certifying that the works have been carried out in line with modern Building Regulations. Please note that it is illegal for anyone to do any work to a domestic wiring installation that is not Part 'P' registered as far as building regulations is concerned.

- **Plastering** – Timescale 7 to 14 days – The extent of plastering to your property will depend on the level of works required, and not all of the internal walls and ceilings may need doing. What I will say here is that when I first take possession of a property, I will usually be inclined to spend a little extra time and money doing a re-plaster of the whole property so that it is good for the next 10 to 15 years depending upon wear and tear. This is a personal preference and may or may not suit your property and respective budget. One big tip that I can give you is, if ceilings in the property are cracked and need to be re-plastered, you will be well advised to overboard the ceilings with a new layer of plasterboard which is fixed to the floor joists or ceiling joists as appropriate. This saves a lot of dust and mess by not removing the existing ceiling and shortens your timeframe for renovation. Always remember that, with plastering, you will need to allow a period of a few days or more for the plaster to dry out before you can start painting. This is essential, otherwise you will end up with discolouration of the paint finish, or, worse, cracking of the new plaster coat.

You should also prioritise the order of the rooms that you want re-plastering, with particular focus on the kitchen and bathroom areas if you are due to install a new bathroom suite or kitchen fitments. This will allow the plasterwork to dry out nicely and permit the tradesmen to continue with work once the plastering team have moved onto another part of the property. A good tip that I learnt from a very experienced plasterer was to ensure that any joints between new sheets of plasterboard are covered with board bonding and scrim cloth. The benefit of this is to ensure that the boards stay firmly fixed together and you don't end up with the traditional hairline cracking to the joint area. To me, this not only looks unsightly, it also defeats the objective of plastering the area in the first place if you are going to have to rake out the joint, fill it with Polyfilla, sand it down and then decorate it. It is a big personal frustration that plasterers allow this to happen; however, by the time it shows up on the job, they will more than likely have left with their money and you will be left with the problem. I do not accept that this shrinkage cracking should be par for the course, and I would say that if a plasterer does not accept putting scrim cloth and board bonding on the plasterboard joints on your projects, then you get another plasterer!

- **Installation of the new kitchen and/or bathroom** – Timescale 7 to 14 days – Once the property has been plastered, you can begin to install the kitchen and bathroom. One school of thought is to always opt for kitchens which come ready assembled so they are easier to fit on site. This is good logic, however you will need to make a decision based on your budget and timescale as to what is feasible for you. Your bathroom suite should really be a white, three-piece suite comprising bath, toilet and wash basin. These can be readily obtained from trade suppliers and are not expensive. I encourage you to go for pressed-steel baths rather than acrylic; the latter flex too much once weight is applied to them, and this causes a lot more stress on the silicone sealant, which could become loose and lead to water leaks at a later date. I also strongly suggest that you go for the best-quality silicone you can find for the bathroom installation (you will know it's the best-quality as you won't believe the price of it compared to the cheap stuff!), so that you can be more certain that you won't have water leaks from the bathroom which will cause you more hassle than you can believe!

- **Timberwork** – Timescale 3 to 10 days – Hopefully, your chosen property will not require complete replacement of the door frames, architrave and skirting boards, so any new timberwork which is required will only be matching the existing where it is missing or rotten, and the installation of new internal doors. I would suggest that you delay the installation of any new timberwork until such time as the plasterwork has completely dried out, otherwise you run the risk of the timber, which is dried in a kiln, absorbing some of the additional moisture in the air (as the plaster dries) which leads to the timber warping! This is not ideal, as it will more than likely need to be replaced. You can help the drying out process using dehumidifiers, but be careful that you do not dry the plaster too quickly (with the use of heat, for example) or it will definitely crack.

- **Decoration** – Timescale 7 to 14 days – The decoration of the property should be one of the last jobs that is performed on the property. If you have had any new plastering done, I would advise that you first cover the new plaster with a 50/50 mix of water and trade emulsion paint, which will be quickly absorbed by the new plaster but will not crack it. If you apply paint straight onto the new plaster, it will inevitably crack which will involve further work in the form of filling, sanding and repairing the cracks to your lovely newly-plastered wall. I would also suggest that the decoration scheme needs to be kept as simple as possible, with magnolia and white applied to the walls and ceilings respectively. Trade paint is not expensive and will provide a good cover for you. Ultimately, you will probably end up giving the walls and ceilings three coats of paint if you have new plasterwork: a 50/50 base layer followed by two coats of undiluted emulsion, which will provide a good cover and leave the room fresh and appealing to the widest possible audience. You should also consider the use of white gloss paint to timberwork as it will be easier to clean in the future and it looks good.

- **Finishing touches** – Timescale 1 to 5 days – The finishing touches to your property will be things like the installation of the ironmongery to doors, lamp shades to lights, and new carpet and vinyl in the appropriate areas. This will make the property desirable and ensure it looks homely once complete. I suggest that you use good quality, hard-wearing carpet throughout which will provide excellent wear during your tenants' occupation. Also use the same colour throughout to keep costs down.

The above gives you a comprehensive order in which to undertake the works to the property and will ensure that the various tradesmen are not falling over one another on site which can in itself cause problems! For the average 3-bedroom, 2-storey terraced property, which is the staple diet of the property investor, you can expect your renovation process to take no longer than four weeks to complete. You will need to have an upfront discussion with your builder and various trades people about how they want to be paid for their work. They may want paying weekly, or at the end of the job, but at no point should you be giving them money upfront for their proposed work. If they require materials to start the job and do not want to be out of pocket for them, then the best thing to do is get them to order the materials, you pay for them and you get them delivered to site so that you have ownership of them. There are many horror stories about people who have trusted a rogue builder and, to their detriment, have been ripped off for several thousands of pounds.

When working with builders and tradesmen, ensure that your attitude towards them is in alignment with your expectations. What do I mean by this? Well, the best way to explain is via some examples. Fred is a rookie investor whom I know through operating in the same area as him. He has a belief that you cannot trust anyone and that all builders are out to rip him off in any way possible. Unsurprisingly, this has been his experience over the last three projects I have known him talk about, where he has spent thousands of pounds unnecessarily by employing the wrong tradespeople and not building long-term relationships with reliable workmen. This is all because of his mistrust of builders and tradespeople.

Let's contrast this with Bradley who is a professional investor who has worked hard to build a team of reliable trades people who he is able to supply with regular work as he spends his time identifying good deals and finding money rather than trying to save a few pounds here and there by working on the properties himself. He was quick to establish a template for the renovations with his builder, which meant everyone knew what to expect, and there was little room for surprises or changes in specification along the way. This in turn led to the builder and various trades people working seamlessly together on site and structuring the order of works efficiently so each project was completed on time and within budget allowing them to move onto the next property. This approach of treating his team as trustworthy until they prove otherwise has served him well and allowed him to save lots of time and money over the last two years of building his buy-to-let portfolio.

I would like to wrap this chapter up by touching on the merits of building a good local team who can handle all your renovations. When you work with people who are good at what they do, you will find your projects progress smoothly, on budget and on time. This is essential as delays on projects can lead to frustrations and, more importantly, an increase in your costs, which will impact your bottom line. If you are a new investor, I would encourage you to just start with your first project and seek recommendations for the people you are likely to be working with, including a trusted builder, electrician and plumber. You can find good recommendations from such organisations as BNI or other breakfast networking events where people regularly can vouch for the work undertaken by those present in the room. This can help you to build successful long-term relationships with people, which will serve you well both now and in the future.

project will be a huge learning curve for you, please do not beat yourself up if things go wrong as, ultimately, there will be hurdles and hiccups along the way which will require some time and money to address. You can ensure that you do not cost yourself a fortune by having the property fully surveyed and getting a timber and damp report done before you buy it. I would also only consider a project that is scruffy inside and really wants just a light refurbishment, i.e. replacement of the kitchen and bathroom and a coat of paint throughout, as this will ensure you do not take on too much and face bigger bills if something unknown crops up on site.

A final word on working with builders and tradesmen is this: make sure they are committed to your project and are not trying to juggle it with lots of other jobs. This can cause a huge amount of frustration if they leave site after only doing half a day's work or they are away from your project for days or weeks at a time. If you find this happening, I would suggest a frank conversation with your builder is required and, if he doesn't change his approach, then you may have to consider letting him go and getting someone else on board to finish the job. Remember, it is your investment and no-one will look after your money like you.

All in all, if you follow the tips given in this chapter, you will find that renovating properties to build your portfolio is a rewarding and exciting experience, which will create value and give good-quality properties which tenants and buyers will take off your hands quickly. Start small and build your way up to bigger projects as your experience and financial situation improves and you will be safe.

CHAPTER NINE

Running it as a Business

By the time you have got to this chapter, I hope to have instilled in you the importance of being a professional investor and the massive benefits of behaving as such. There is nothing more important when we are talking about investing tens of thousands of pounds and taking on lots of debt in the form of mortgages in order to purchase properties, than handling the management and running of the properties carefully so that you are well covered in terms of receiving monthly rent and being able to meet the mortgage payments each and every month. Many a seemingly successful investor has caught a cold in terms of taking their eye off the ball and allowing a few void periods here and there to absorb their free cash flow, resulting in them hitting the quick downward spiral of losing money from loss of rent and also not being able to meet the mortgage payments due to lack of funds. Or, they are saddled with properties which quickly deteriorate, as they do not have enough money set aside to cover the maintenance issues as and when they crop up.

I cannot emphasise enough the importance of running this as a business and making sure your properties are always full, that they are looked after, and your rents are paid in full and on time every single month. When rent is not received, you need to chase this up with your tenants to make sure you can make the monthly mortgage payments. When maintenance issues crop up, you need to have enough money set aside in a separate bank account so that you can cover whatever issue needs to be attended to. Failure to do these things will result in the business working against you rather than for you and consuming you in anxiety over how the mortgages will be paid and how to fund the repairs required along the way.

So, how do we run all this as a business? Well, one of the key things that I would suggest you do as an action point after you have completed the reading of this book would be to read *The E-Myth Revisited* by Michael Gerber, which I can honestly say is one of the best books I have ever read. I only wish that I had read it five years earlier than I did! However, *The E-Myth Revisited* explores the importance of having systems in your business, which will allow it to run effectively without a huge amount of involvement from yourself. Sounds ideal? Well, it's pretty good; however there is still a lot of work to do upfront before you will be in this very fortunate and rewarding position.

In order to fast-track your success however, I will give you some of my best guidance in terms of running all this as a business so that it is a rewarding and profitable enterprise rather than something that you despise. Remember that you are more than likely getting into property investment as a way to get away from the 9-5 work day and build something that will last you well into your pensionable age as well as giving you a comfortable retirement, so it's important to do this right from the start rather than building an empire on quicksand.

One of the most important words that I want to introduce you to in property is the word 'leverage'. If you are unsure what this means, the best definition I can give you is 'the ability to do a lot with a little'. We all have 24 hours in a day, and therefore it is important that we use this time correctly. Trying to be the one person who does all the maintenance, renovation and management of your properties is going to be exhausting and unfulfilling in the long-term. You will end up like one rookie investor in my area, Bob, who has a couple of properties, but does all the maintenance himself. I once met him for coffee on a Monday morning and immediately regretted asking him how his weekend was as he went into great detail over how he had spent two days fixing a leaking pipe under a bath! The reason it took so long was because it was concealed by a decorative tiled enclosure, which he had to break into, and then re-tile in intricate detail before the job was finished. This is a nightmare scenario and one that I am personally grateful to not be in!

We need to leverage our time by employing the services of professional people who will do some of the work for us, whilst we benefit from maximum reward. One of the key players here will be the letting agent that we choose to work with to manage the properties. Some rookies make the mistake of saying they will manage the properties themselves in order to save themselves paying 10%-15%

of the rental income to the letting agents, however this is folly in my experience.

A good letting agent is worth their weight in gold and you want to work with key people who will help you to run this as a business and manage your properties carefully for you. How do you pick a good agent? This is a great question and one that I would offer the following guidance on:

- First of all, visit all the letting agents in the area you are choosing to invest in. Ask them the questions that follow and make a note of how they respond to you. There are huge differences between letting agents, and in my experience of visiting many towns and cities around the UK, there is generally only one letting agent in each area that you want to work with. The key is finding them and using them!

- Ask the letting agent if they are an investor themselves. This question really separates the wheat from the chaff, as many letting agents aren't investors and, if they claim they are, they are rarely following the procedures outlined in this book. Those that are understand the impact of voids and expensive maintenance on properties and will be more pro-active than those agents who are just letting other people's properties and do not understand the importance of cash flow.

- Take copies of a street map with you and a green and red highlighter pen. Ask each agent you visit to highlight the areas of the town where they have high demand with the green highlighter and the areas of town that you should avoid with the red highlighter. You want good-quality properties rather than cheap houses, which are in rough areas, which you will end up paying your tenants to stay in!

- Ask the agent the following question to test demand for property types: *"If I were to bring you a property which you could rent out in a heartbeat, what would it be and where would it be?"* This qualifies the property type and area that is in demand and helps you buy to this demand.

- You would also be well placed to enquire who the local trades people are that they use, and if they would be happy to provide a recommendation for a builder, electrician and plumber as you would like some assistance in renovating properties to a good standard for lettings purposes.

- Finally, ask the letting agent if any of their landlords are looking to sell their properties or get out of the business. This can be a great source of leads for you! You can also incentivise them by advising that you will leave the properties with them if you buy them.

Once you have spoken to all the letting agents in the area, it will be fairly obvious who you want to be working with to manage your properties. Ask them what systems they have to manage the properties, how the rent will be sent to you and what they require to start managing the property upfront. Set a standard for the system you want to work with and be rigorous in your demands with the letting agents on how you want your property to be managed. The time saved here will be huge! One great tip I have for you is to ensure that you provide the letting agent with an authorised limit to which they can instruct any maintenance jobs without referring back to you. This makes things quite efficient from all sides as the letting agent can get on with the management and maintenance works without the need to contact you, which will hopefully make things run smoothly and avoid unnecessary hold-ups, which can sometimes cause frustration with tenants.

Once your managing agent is in place, they should be responsible for finding and vetting tenants, issuing the Assured Shorthold Tenancy (AST) document and inventory, and handling check-in as well as dealing with the tenant and any benefit claims they may need to do in order to secure Housing Benefit from the Council to pay your rent. As an aside here, many people get nervous about dealing with tenants on benefits and refuse to take them due to the stigma associated with them, which apparently makes them bad tenants. As someone who deals almost exclusively with tenants on housing benefit, I can assure you that this is not the case, and many other professional investors I associate with are more than happy to take people on housing benefit and report that they are great tenants.

Make sure that your letting agent is doing a good job of managing the properties by ensuring the monthly rent is paid on time and in full to you (minus their lettings fee). If there are any times when your tenants hand in notice to leave the property, this is when the letting agent must step in and ensure the property is advertised quickly and filled asap so that void periods do not become a problem for you. Voids are periods where there is no-one in occupation at the property, and you are the one responsible for paying the mortgage payment! This is not the objective of being a property investor and therefore a new tenant must be found quickly or the mortgage payment will be coming out of your pocket.

I need to make you aware that, if you as the landlord are giving notice to your tenants to leave the property, you have to give them two months' notice. The best way to do this is via the use of a Section 21 notice, which you must sign and serve to the tenant in accordance with English law. Some rookie landlords serve the Section 21 notice to their tenants at the start of the tenancy, but I think this gives the wrong impression and sets an expectation that the tenant will inevitably fail and will need to leave the property. To my mind, it makes perfect sense to have good-quality properties with good tenants who choose to stay with you for long periods of time and pay their rent every month.

When it comes to renting properties, you need to be aware of some golden rules of letting in order to protect your investment. These are:

1. Before any tenant moves into your property, they must be required to sign an AST agreement which details all their responsibilities as well as your own as a landlord. If you want to make your life easy, make sure they sign the agreement as well as initialling every page in the bottom corner. This protects you, as should things get contentious in the future, the tenant cannot claim to have not seen the page in the tenancy agreement where it details the rent they have to pay and the terms they have to comply with! Never, ever, allow a

tenant to move into a property without a signed AST, as the minimum period of occupancy is six months by law (even without an AST). If they move in and never pay you a penny in rent, then you will not be able to evict the tenant any earlier than six months and the courts will always favour the tenant rather than the landlord as you will be deemed to know better.

2. Always do an inspection of the property a month after the tenant moves in. You or the letting agent can do this, but it is important to ensure that the inspection takes place. The reason for doing it after one month rather than quarterly as suggested by most people is because you will be able to determine quite quickly whether or not there is likely to be a problem with the tenant. You will also get some idea of how they live and, if there are apparent problems, you can draw the tenant's attention to the AST initially to try to sort out any problems. If this doesn't work, then you can serve them notice to get them out of the property at the end of the six-month term. This just gives you a certain amount of peace of mind and prevents problems spiralling out of control and the landlord and tenant relationship disintegrating.

3. Always protect the tenant's deposit (if you take one) with one of the approved deposit protection schemes and let the tenant know immediately where the deposit has been lodged or protected. There are quite severe consequences for not doing so including paying a fine of three times the

deposit to the tenant. Clearly, no landlord wants to find themselves in this situation. Your letting agent should be able to guide you further on this if you are in any way unsure of what is required; however, these are good words of wisdom, based on my experience, which will keep you safe.

Once you have been renting your property out for a period of months, you should be checking your progress on a regular basis to ensure that the property is performing as it should. I certainly recommend you do a monthly check to ensure all rents have been received so that you can chase any outstanding money immediately. This might not be too difficult with one or two properties, however, with a more substantial portfolio, it can be harder to track the rents coming in. I also recommend that you keep an eye on the amount of money you are spending on maintenance on each property over the course of a year. This needs to be monitored closely as more than likely it will show you which of the properties in your portfolio are the 'problem children' and may need to be sold or have action taken in order to bring them in line with other properties and prevent them becoming a drain on your business.

You should also be setting aside some rent every month in a separate account in order to cover any maintenance issues that crop up over the course of the year. There will always be annual expenses, such as the buildings insurance policy and the gas safety certificate, however, there may be other issues that crop up which need to be addressed and you want to make sure that you are not short of money to cover these items of work. This is when investors start to get into problems by running their portfolio too tightly and spending all of the income rather than setting some aside to cover expenses. In particular, you will need to monitor peak times of expenditure such as winter when you can expect more boiler breakdowns due to increased use in the colder weather.

Employing the services of a good-quality accountant can be of huge benefit to you and I cannot emphasise enough the importance of working with a professional here who understands how property investing works. In addition, employing the services of a property tax advisor can be well worth it in the initial stages so that you can understand how to set your portfolio up in the correct manner to protect your investment for the future and pass it onto your family once the final curtain closes. Many rookies work hard to build their portfolio, only to pass the majority of it onto the taxman because they didn't plan ahead sufficiently!

Once you have established a system for buying, renovating and letting your first property, I would encourage you to look carefully at each stage of the process so that you can see which bits are working well and which will benefit from further improvements. The more you pay attention to, and hone, your systems, the more effective they will become and the more efficient your operation. This will in turn add to your bottom line and give you a much better return on investment. It will also give you greater confidence in how to further expand your business and start buying more and more properties which will ultimately lead to you receiving more and more investment income from your properties which will eventually buy you financial freedom (where you have more money coming in than you need to cover your monthly expenses). This is a great place to be. Here you have time and freedom to do what you want to do, when you want to do it. I can tell you from personal experience that it is a very liberating place to be and certainly reduces a lot of personal stress from working in a job environment, which you may not enjoy at all!

CHAPTER TEN

Conclusion

Congratulations on making it this far and well done on your commitment to being the best in the business! I am both pleased and proud that our paths have crossed and I have been able to impart at least some of my knowledge to you which I hope you have found to be of great benefit. I am very confident that, by following the guidance contained within this book, you will make the right choices as a property investor and build your business in the right way, which will not only help a lot of other people but will also benefit you immensely.

By now, I am sure you have seen the benefits of running your property business as a true professional and not as a rookie in your approach. I have to say that, without a working knowledge of property investing yourself and surrounding yourself with a team who supports you in your endeavours, you will be setting yourself up for failure as there is too much to do and know for one person to do it all on their own. I am a firm believer in being a team player rather than a lone ranger.

One of the biggest things I have learnt throughout my journey is the incredible power of a third party in your life in the form of a mentor who can hold you accountable in your endeavours to ensure you will be successful in what you are doing. Since I discovered the power of a mentor, I have sought to employ them in all areas of my life including health, business and relationships. There is no shame in asking for help and support in your journey, as without it, you are learning to do things the hard way. I will give you an example of my own experience learning to be an author. In 2012, I decided to write my first book. As I regard writing as one of my hobbies, I picked up and put down this project over the course of two years, and still didn't finish the book! Contrast that with my performance once I got a mentor on board to assist with writing. Not only did the book get completely rewritten, the first draft was completed within five weeks and the book was ready for publishing within three months! This is a stark contrast to taking two years to not write a book!

I have also had this experience in business, where I spent 18 months building a business only to realise that I was doing it for all the wrong reasons and it was deeply unfulfilling. My mentor encouraged me to look deeply at the reasons why I was doing this and ultimately I decided to close the business, as it was not making me happy. As a coincidence, the business also wasn't making a lot of money, which shows that when your heart is not in it, it will not perform or do what you want it to do!

So, for those of you who are looking to build their business both quickly and profitably, I have to say that the best way I know to achieve this is through employing the services of a mentor who has been there time and time again and from whose experience you can learn rather than making all the mistakes yourself. Where do you find a good mentor? Well, that's a good question! In my experience there are a lot of people in property who claim to be mentors, however their knowledge, experience and 'success' is questionable. I have even known people with very little property experience, and who are holding a small property portfolio which is killing them, to offer their services to new investors as a mentor! To my mind, nothing could be worse for the poor unsuspecting investor who wants to start and grow their business but is receiving advice and guidance from someone who doesn't know what they are talking about!

I would also encourage you not to have anyone who is a friend as your mentor as this relationship inevitably doesn't work. A mentor has to be able to have frank and open conversations with you, which a friend may not be willing to have as they run the risk of upsetting you or the relationship. Your mentor's job is not to like you; it is more that they are there to help and protect you a lot and make sure you are not making silly mistakes which will cost you dearly. I know one gentleman who chose a close friend of his who claimed to already be 'in property' to be his mentor – this simple mistake ultimately cost him over £22,000 in a botched renovation on the first property he bought, which he paid too much for. It turns out his friend was an estate agent. Not quite a professional property investor!

I often use the example of going into property without a mentor as driving a very fast car down the motorway having only had one driving lesson; sooner or later there is going to be a very nasty accident! This is not my wish for anyone, and seeking the counsel of people who know what they are doing is absolutely invaluable for you. Hand-in-hand with this is the requirement to have a very strong team of professionals around you in the form of a great solicitor, mortgage broker, accountant, tax advisor, financial planner (not financial advisor – there is a difference), and build team to complete your renovations on your properties. Finding these people is not easy and can take lots of work and some bitter experiences until you have got it right!

For those of you that know you want to build your business in the right manner, then I would encourage you to visit my website (www.assafeashouses.com) where I have provided several resources for you as a property investor to help you build your business. I would also like to extend the offer of help and assistance to you wherever I can to help you along your way. I greatly appreciate you taking the time to read this book and if I can return the favour by giving you access to my own personal power team who help and assist me in the running of my own business, then I certainly will do.

As part of my everyday activities, I am still very much involved in building my property portfolio whilst also pursuing other interests, which I find greatly rewarding, such as public speaking where I help and support others to get started on their journey in property. This is without a doubt one of the things that I enjoy the most in my professional life, and whilst I am protective of the time that I allocate to business outside of my family life, I do occasionally have space in my diary to mentor and coach budding property professionals to achieve their goals and dreams. If you think this may be appropriate for you, then please contact me via my website and I will come back to you asap. As I also work with a great group of property professionals who may also be able to assist you, this may also be an option if I do not have the time available to personally work with you.

There may be some readers who are looking for a joint venture specialist if they already have some property deals on the table but are unsure what to do with them. If you want to take these forward, or learn in greater depth how to build a property sourcing business in the right way so you can earn a good income whilst you practice your craft, then I would encourage you to get in touch via the website where I have some great resources to help you out.

One thing I will encourage you to do is to absolutely take action on the contents of these pages as the rewards for doing so will be massive. You have come a long way through the reading of the pages of this book and taken a huge leap forward in your knowledge. The last thing I want is for you to put this book down and for all this information to become a thing of the past. So many people 'never get around' to taking action on the things they have learnt and then wonder why their life is dull and unfulfilling. I know you are different, and given the chance, you have the power to change your life for the better. I would encourage you to reflect back on chapter one of this book and ask yourself the question again of 'why are you doing this?' and remind yourself of your answer. Please do not let this education experience be a thing of the past but take every step you can to make your dreams a reality.

There is nothing on earth that can stop a determined person; a person who has a strong why and the desire to see it through to completion. Those are the types of people we all admire as a society; the underdog in the film who looks like they may be beaten time and again is always the one that pulls through and makes a success of their endeavour. I encourage you to emulate the same success in your life and to underpin your activities in property with a strong why and desire to do good in this life. If you are the sort of person that wants to help others and give to charity, then you will be able to do so in spectacular fashion once you have taken care of your own personal situation first and foremost. I cannot emphasise how important this is as I see many, many people put the needs of others before their own as some example of saintliness, but in reality this is a show of martyrdom – they end up unhappy and resenting the very people they are trying to help in the first place! Not a good situation to be in!

I therefore encourage you to make a written note of your 'why' and carry this with you everywhere and put it in a few places that are visible to you such as the fridge and the bathroom mirror. This will help to keep you going when the chips are down and you are encountering hurdles in your progress. There will undoubtedly be some rejection and some heartache in the pursuit of your dreams, however with a strong why backing your every move, then you will undoubtedly achieve whatever it is you want in life.

As the saying goes, 'If you don't build your dream, someone else will hire you to help build theirs'. I do not know any other industry where you and I can receive the sorts of benefits that are forthcoming from running a successful property business and which has less barriers to entry than property. I love how fair the business is, and regardless of your age, gender or social status, with the right mindset and application of the right knowledge, you cannot help but be successful. The industry does not have a prejudice against anyone who doesn't have money or indeed doesn't have the 'right contacts'; only those who don't learn in the right manner and who are not prepared to invest in themselves. So take action and watch the rewards for your efforts come flooding in.

I wish you the very best in your journey towards success.

Much love and best wishes,

Silas.

About The Author

Silas J. Lees MRICS has always had a keen interest in property, which evolved from helping his parents renovate many properties as he was growing up. He pursued this interest throughout his career starting his working life as an estate agent whilst studying part-time to be a Building Surveyor at Wolverhampton University. In 2007, he started his career in property investment and bought his first investment property in December of that year, shortly before the biggest recession in global history! Since then, he has continued to build and develop his portfolio throughout a downwards market whilst also helping other people secure their financial future by doing the same through personal mentoring and public speaking. He lives in the historic Ironbridge in Shropshire and spends his time pursuing his passions, which include travelling, reading, writing and helping others follow their dreams. His ambition currently is to be an international property investor!

Worksheet

My Why Is:

....

....

....

....

....

....

....

....

....

....

....

Think carefully about your why. It is a worthy investment of your time. Is what you have written powerful enough to help you overcome your fears whilst putting the time and effort in to achieve a monthly investment income that will pay for your lifestyle? If not, think deeply about what you care about in life and what you would do if you had the free time to be able to do it. There are no right or wrong answers here; just what you want out of your life.

My Currently Hourly Rate Exercise

1. Monthly Take Home Pay: _____

2. Number of hours worked per week: _____

3. Total monthly hours worked (multiple figure in 2 by 4.33): _____

4. Monthly pay divided by working hours: _____

5. Current hourly rate of pay is: _____

6. Monthly income I need to achieve from property in order to be financially free is: _____ Date I will achieve this by: _____

Be realistic about this. We would all love £100,000pcm investment income in two weeks, however the point of declaring the monthly income you require here is to give you a sensible and achievable target to hit. Once you have hit this target and you have the option to give up your job, you can then set the next goal to achieve a higher level of income if this is what you desire.

If you want it badly enough, you'll find a way. If you don't, you'll find an excuse.

What accountability structure is in place to make sure you achieve your goals?

Live Your Gift To The World

Investment Returns Worksheet

Example:

Monthly Rental Income	£650.00
Mortgage costs per month	£375.00
£100,000 x 75% =	£75,000
£75,000 x 6% =	£4,500
£4,500 divided by 12 =	£375
Lettings Fee @ 15% of rent =	£97.50
Repairs & Maintenance Budget @ 10% of rent =	£65.00
Contingency @ 5% of rent =	£32.50
Total Investment Income	£80 per calendar month

How to work out the Investment Income:

i) Monthly Rental Income for property   £

Minus the following costs:

ii) Mortgage Costs per month   £

Purchase Price x 75% = Mortgage Amount

Mortgage Amount x 6% = Annual Mortgage Interest

Annual Mortgage Interest divided by 12 = Monthly mortgage cost

iii) Lettings Fee @15% of rental income (i) x 0.15)   £

iv) Repairs & Maintenance Budget
@ 10% of rental income   £

v) Contingency @ 5% of rent   £

Gives you the following total investment income

vi) Total Investment Income - per calendar month.   £

Blank Investment Returns Worksheet

i) Monthly Rental Income for property   £

Minus the following costs:

ii) Mortgage Costs per month   £

£   x 75% = £

£   x 6% = £

£   divided by 12 = £

iii) Lettings Fee @15% of rental income (i) x 0.15   £

iv) Repairs & Maintenance Budget
     @ 10% of rental income   (i) x 0.10   £

v) Contingency @ 5% of rent   (i) x 0.05   £

Gives you the following total investment income

(vi) Total Investment Income - per calendar month.   £

Choosing My Investment Area

The Following is a summary of information contained within Chapter Three of the book.

Step One: Open two tabs on your browser, both with Rightmove on them.

Step Two: On the first tab, go into Rightmove 'For Sale' and search for 3 bedroom terraced properties up to a maximum of £100,000. Consider towns and areas of cities that are in the North of England (North of Birmingham) and South Wales as sensible areas for investment.

Step Three: Your search results should yield at least 65 properties for sale otherwise you need to pick a different area.

Step Four: Pick five properties at random from the selection that has come up in your search results. At this stage, we are not worried about whether or not they require work; as long as they are 3 bedroom terraced properties in a particular town, then that is ok.

Step Five: Now go to the second tab in your web browser and look at Rightmove 'To Rent' in the same area that you searched for properties 'For Sale' in. Search for the same property type, but do not put a limit on the rental figures. Use the map function to narrow in on a property which is comparable to the one you have found which is for sale. This will give you a good idea of the likely rental figure for the property you are looking at.

Step Six: Repeat Step Five for the five properties you have identified for sale and then use the rental figures to run the investment returns calculation we reviewed earlier. Work out each and every calculation on a separate sheet of A4 paper by hand.

Step Seven: Once you have worked out your five investment calculations for the first area you have chosen, choose another nine towns or areas of cities in the UK to explore and do the same exercise with these, so that you will have done 50 investment calculations in total. **Do not shortcut this step as you could miss an incredible investment area and not even know it.**

Step Eight: Review the 10 areas and you will see that three of those areas will work better than the other seven. Therefore, discard the seven and focus on the three areas where you can consider investing once you have been to visit them and see if they are the kind of areas you want to buy properties in.

Step Nine: Once you have the three proposed areas that work on a strictly numbers basis, you will then need to plan to visit them all. Visit them on three weekends in quick succession and take a good drive around the areas to see if they feel right to you. I always imagine someone close to me when I am driving around the areas and I ask myself the question: *"Would I be happy to let them live there?"* If the answer is no, then I would move on to the next area.

Step Ten: Once you have visited the three areas, you will have a very good idea about which one you will want to invest in. Your task is to then visit your investment area at least once a month to continue to build up your local knowledge and become the local expert on residential property investment in your area.

Step Nine: The Three Areas I have chosen to visit are:

(i) _____ Date I plan to visit: _____
(ii) _____ Date I plan to visit: _____
(iii) _____ Date I plan to visit: _____

Step Ten: The Area I have chosen to invest in is:

_____

_____

I confirm that I have undertaken the full 50 investment calculations suggested in the above exercise:

Signed: (i) _____

Date: _____

Please visit **www.assafeashouses.com** to download a copy of this worksheet.

Notes:

....

....

....

....

....

....

....

....

....

....

....

....

....

....

....

....

....

....

Notes:

Notes:

Notes:

Printed in Great Britain
by Amazon